‖‖‖‖‖‖‖‖‖‖‖‖‖‖‖‖‖‖‖‖‖‖‖

W9-BVE-985

Lincoln Christian College

Bots. Do you not heare him? you marre our labour,
Keep your Cabines: you do assist the storme.

Gonz. Nay, good be patient.

Bots. When the Sea is: hence, what cares these roa-
rers for the name of King? to Cabine: silence: trouble
vs not.

Gon. Good, yet remember whom thou hast aboord.

Bots. None that I more loue then my selfe. You are
a Counsellor, if you can command these Elements to silence, and worke the peace of the present, wee will not
hand a rope more, vse your authoritie: If you cannot,
giue thankes you haue liu'd so long, and make your
selfe readie in your Cabine for the mischance of the
houre, if it so hap. Cheerely good hearts: out of our
way I say.   *Exit.*

Gon. I haue great comfort from this fellow: methinks
he hath no drowning marke vpon him, his complexion
is perfect Gallowes: stand fast good Fate to his hanging, make the rope of his destiny our cable, for our
owne doth little aduantage: If he be not borne to bee
hang'd, our case is miserable.   *Exit.*

Enter Boteswaine.

Bots. Downe with the top-Mast: yare, lower, lower,
Bring her to Try with Maine-course. A plague ——
                          Enter Sebastian, Anthonio & Gonzalo.
A cry within.

An't we are meerely cheated of our liues by drunkards,
This wide-chopt-rascall, would thou mightst lye drowning the washing of ten Tides.

Gonz. Hee'l be hang'd yet,
Though euery drop of water sweare against it,
And gape at widst to glut him. *A confused noyse within.*
Mercy on vs.
We split, we split, Farewell my wife, and children,
Farewell brother: we split, we split, we split.

Anth. Let's all sinke with' King

Seb. Let's take leaue of him.   *Exit.*

Gonz. Now would I giue a thousand furlongs of Sea,
for an Acre of barren ground: Long heath, Browne
firs, any thing; the wills aboue be done, but I would
faine dye a dry death.   *Exit.*

Scena Secunda.

Enter Prospero and Miranda.

Mira. If by your Art (my deerest father) you haue
Put the wild waters in this Rore; alay them:
The skye it seemes would powre down stinking pitch,
But that the Sea, mounting to th' welkins cheeke,
Dashes the fire out. Oh! I haue suffered
With those that I saw suffer: A braue vessell

(Who

A

WASN'T

SHAKESPEARE

SOMEONE

ELSE?

NEW EVIDENCE
IN THE VERY WORDS
OF THE BARD HIMSELF
ABOUT HIS TRUE IDENTITY

By Ralph L. Tweedale

The Shakespeare Oxford Society

To the memory of

EDWARD DeVERE,

17th Earl of Oxford

1550-1604

Library of Congress catalog card number 78-147247

©1966, 1971 Ralph L. Tweedale

PREFACE

This book is not a Protestant thesis to be nailed to the sanctuary door. Rather, it is an offering to the reader who wants to see for himself what evidence Shakespeare left behind to tell us who he really was. Those who are satisfied to accept the pronouncements of "authority" on the question can listen to the many eloquent pleaders for "Shaxper" of Stratford. From behind the bastions of professional scholarship, so much presumption and assumption about him has issued and re-issued that critical analysis of what are stated as facts is rarely heard. Those voices that do rise in opposition are shouted down with scorn and ridicule but no directly relevant answers.

Instead of partisan pleading, I have endeavored to present the evidence without rhetoric or invective and with only such explanation and background as is needed to place it in the overall context. Its form, in the old typography, may look formidable at first blush, but with a little patience it quickly becomes as familiar as modern text forms. In presenting the material chronologically, its initial impact is weakened. I trust that the reader will not thereby be tempted to dismiss it without going on to the meatier sections. The progressive development of the Shakespearean ingenuity is one of the more interesting aspects of the picture.

For leads to valuable background material, I wish to thank Mr. William P. Walker. For his encouragement and that of the late Mr. Walter Lattman I am much in debt. And without the efficient secretarial assistance of Mrs. Helen Jackson I could not have begun this undertaking.

The views expressed in these pages are, of course, my own even though erected upon a foundation so firmly laid by others. The Shakespeare Oxford Society in carrying out its objective of publishing the results of research in this field neither endorses nor refutes this author's conclusions.

R. L. T.

CONTENTS

****

Oh learne to read what silent love hath writ

To heare with eies belongs to love's fine wit

Sonnet 23

CHAPTER 1

THE QUESTION STATED

Why have the works of William Shakespeare generated such a current of derivative literature that in a single year, three and a half centuries after his supposed death, a total of 1,564 items of literature were published and indexed dealing directly with that subject?[1] Surely no other genius, whether in literature, drama, or any other branch of the arts, can match that record.

1. *Shakespeare Quarterly*—Vol. XVIII, p. 207

Why does the specter of a concealed authorship continue to lurk in the literary boondocks; occasionally floating into view to set off a flurry of refutation and reassurance for his faithful devotees?

The answer to the first question lies, of course , in the man's exceptional talents. And strangely enough, the second question is bound up in those same talents, although exercised in a way and to an extent which is hard to believe possible. Unseen down the centuries, there has lain buried in these masterpieces of literature the most ingenious visual devices, which by the use of a very simple key to their recognition, identify the name of the true author and tie it unequivocally to the pseudonym William Shakespeare.

Our language develops in a variety of ways as new concepts come on the scene and require labels. Old words are borrowed to identify the innovations and before long have lost their original significance entirely. The motor car converted the noun park to a verb. Not long ago tuning was done only to pianos, not engines or radios. Prominent figures lend their names to a vogue and by the next generation have become only adjectives. We have Georgian architecture, Victorian morality, Louis XV furniture and Edwardian literature. The list is long, but of all the figures of modern history only Elizabeth The First left her name as a symbol not merely of an age, but of a race. The latter years of the sixteenth century are known only as the Elizabethan times. How do we speak of that race of giants which included Shakespeare, Raleigh, Drake, Bacon, Burleigh and Coke except as Elizabethans? The devotion of these men to their Queen and country transformed England into a world power and elevated the English language from a mere tool of communication to an instrument of the arts.

The era has been a favorite for scholars, critics and writers. Its characters and chronicles bear an aura of attractive mystery unique among all periods of modern times. The Virgin Queen has been linked romantically to any number of her favorite nobles in as many historical novels. The Elizabethan poet-dramatists have been researched on a continuing basis for years. Rooted in the rich loam of the period's enigmatic records is a lush stand of derivative writings of all kinds—history, novel, criticism, interpretation. The books, if gathered all together, would fill a small public library.

By far the richest part of the garden is the Shakespearean section. If Shakespeare's ideas about women, horses, hawking, boating, law, religion, war, or any of a hundred other themes have not been authoritatively treated in the last few decades it is not too early to expect a new critical work on the subject. Critics have devoted a career to deciding which plays are canonical and what portions of the works are by other hands. The problem of dating the plays and determining the true sequence of the Sonnets has deeply concerned the ablest scholars and critics alike. The reconstruction of the events of printing and proofreading of the first folio has resulted in a far larger printing and proofreading job than the first folio itself.[2] The exploration of the hidden ciphers and codes which purportedly have been discovered in Shakespeare has merited the attention of the most renowned cryptographers. Even the portraits of Shakespeare have been subjected to rigorous X-ray, infra-red and other scientific examinations.

It is no surprise that a titan of the arts like Shakespeare should inspire literary criticism and scholarship to the extent of hundreds of volumes and in several languages, and it would be surprising indeed if anything of major significance should have escaped for nearly four centuries the notice of the many students of his works and environment. The Qumran caves by the Dead Sea will yield no manuscripts of this author, nor is it very likely that more relevant spots like the Stratford monument will yield them either. Yet something very significant in the works themselves seems to have been entirely overlooked.

2. *The Printing and Proofreading of the First Folio of Shakespeare,* by Charlton Hinman, Oxford University Press, 1963— 2 Vols.

Through concentration on the purely literary aspects—
meter, endings, imagery and the rest, the other content of
the works has been largely ignored. True, there have been
launched several secret ciphers purporting to show that Francis Bacon, Christopher Marlowe or some other contemporary
was the real author. All seem to have lost their momentum
and fallen to earth long since. What vestige of doubt re-
mained has been expertly wiped away by the Friedmans.[3]
This husband and wife team of American cryptanalysts have,
as a life long hobby, tested each of the ciphers supposed to be
in Shakespeare and found them all invalid. The conclusions
of the man who broke the Japanese diplomatic cipher before
the attack on Pearl Harbor are not to be lightly dismissed.
Further promotion of any of these dubious secret codes in
Shakespeare has been solidly blocked by Colonel and Mrs.
Friedman and any new promotion along similar lines would
meet an almost automatic rejection as already disproven by
their once-for-all analysis.

Is it possible that the Shakespearean works do contain
more than we have heretofore seen in them? Was the Bard
speaking a richer language than we have so far been able to
read? Is there a substantive content beyond what meets the
eye by the usual methods of reading? We know that Shakespeare was fond of extremely belabored puns. Many passages
play on double meanings to a shameless degree and some
scenes carry significance on three different levels of meaning
at once. Lyly and his "euphuists" carried the practice to ri-
diculous excess, going so far as to make all conversation and
repartee an exercise in innuendo and double talk.

This interest in giving their language more than one
meaning took still another form. One of the nearly forgotten
arts of the Elizabethans was the composing of acrostic poetry.
As English literature was coming to its first full fruition
under the matchless hand of Shakespeare, his fellow poets
were not sticking to their knitting. Dissatisfied with mere

3. *The Shakespeare Ciphers Examined*, Cambridge University
Press, 1957

successive lines of straightforward meter and rhyme they had to give their work both a warp and woof. Wide interest fastened upon compositions which could be read not only from left to right but up and down as well. The textile analogy is indeed apropos since "text" and "textile" have a common Latin root, meaning something that is woven.

Here are but four examples (out of who knows how many such?) from Elizabethan times.

The play "Volpone" is preceded by this "argument."

V olpone, childless, rich, feigns sick, despairs,
O ffers his state to hopes of several heirs,
L ies languishing; his Parasite receives
P resents of all, assures, deludes; then weaves
O ther cross plots, which ope themselves, are told.
N ew tricks for safety are sought; they thrive; when, bold,
E ach tempts th' other again, and all are sold.

Here is a eulogy in acrostic form.

A POEM ON SIR P. S.

Perfection peerless, Vertue without pride,
Honour and Learning, linked with highest Love,
Joy of the thought in true discretion tied,
Love of the life that highest honours prove.
  In Angels' arms with heavenly hands embraced
  Paradise pleased, and all the world disgraced

Seek all the world, oh seek and never find,
In earthly mould, the mount of such a m'
Divinest gifts that God or man bestow,
No glory such as of such glory gro' done.
  End of the joys that hath all gr'
  Yet let one weep when all the

The Queen was honored in a series of twenty-six poems like this one.

ACROSTIC

Earth now is green and heaven is blue;
Lively spring which makes all new.
Iolly spring doth enter.
Sweet young sunbeams do subdue
Angry aged winter.
Blasts are mild and seas are calm,
Every meadow flows with balm,
The earth wears all her riches,
Harmonious birds sing such a psalm
As ear and heart bewitches.

Reserve (sweet spring) this nymph of ours,
Eternal garlands of thy flowers,
Green garlands never wasting;
In her shall last our state's fair spring,
Now and forever flourishing,
As long as heaven is lasting.

Sir John Davies.

The following is an example written by Anthony Munday to his patron, Lord Oxford, in 1579:

E xcept I should in freendship seeme ingrate,
D enying duty, where to I am bound;
V ith letting slip your Honour's worthy state,
all assayes, which I have Noble found.
't well I might refrayne to handle pen:
E ncing aye the company of men.

V ertue despayre, let courage come in place,
E xample ne whom Honour doth imbrace.
R egarding e adornd your valiant hart,
E che where by ur deeds of lasting fame:
take God Mars his parte,
e, in Honnor and in name.

The Shakespearean author himself was not above placing acrostics in the margins of verse. A number of instances are known where the acrostic word or words will link in thought directly to the adjacent text. Here are some of the less bawdy examples that others have found in the original edition of the plays.

> *Pro.* Thus haue I ſhund the fire, for feare of burning,
> And drench'd me in the ſea, where I am drown'd.
> I fear'd to ſhew my Father *Iulias* Letter,
> Leaſt he ſhould take exceptions to my loue,
> And with the vantage of mine owne excuſe
> Hath he excepted moſt againſt my loue.
> Oh, how this ſpring of loue reſembleth
> The vncertaine glory of an Aprill day,
> Which now ſhewes all the beauty of the Sun,
> And by and by a clowd takes all away.
> *Pan.* Sir *Protheus*, your Fathers call's for you,
> He is in haſt, therefore I pray you go.

In the first two lines Proteus, one of the two gentlemen of Verona, describes his predicament by the metaphor of warming his "tail" by the fire and then tumbling into the sea. The marginal acrostic reads "TAIL A HOT WASH."

Here in *Titus Adronicus* is an acrostic reference to the stringent sedition laws enacted in Shakespearean times.

> For I haue heard my Grandſier ſay full oft,
> Extremitie of griefes would make men mad.
> And I haue read that *Hecuba* of Troy,
> Ran mad through ſorrow, that made me to feare,
> Although my Lord, I know my noble Aunt,
> Loues me as deare as ere my mother did,
> And would not but in fury fright my youth,
> Which made me downe to throw my bookes, and flie

Notice that the idea is linked to the text by the word "feare" in line 4.

Little of the art survives today and that only in doggerel

sentiment occasionally found on greeting cards. Besides those talented friends who continue to amuse us with their original cards each Christmas, and who sometimes make up an acrostic, there is now a professional printing house selling "individualized" cards with an appropriate sentiment, which, if one reads down the first letters of the lines, what does it spell but THE JOHN JOHNSONS or BETTY AND FRED.

The acrostic as a form of secret writing of course has been elaborated into many varieties besides the obvious marginal type. Its popularity has been somewhat cyclical and seems to be related to the stress and strain of the times. The Hebrew writer of the Book of Lamentations incorporated acrostic messages in his tale of ancient oppression.[4] Centuries later the early Christians based their secret sign of a fish on the initial Greek letters of the five words Jesus-Christ-God-Son-Saviour. They lived under cruel persecution. So we need not wonder at the Elizabethans' interest in acrostics; their times were also marked by intense civil and religious strife held in check by a barbarously despotic government.

We can easily assume that the basic rights which free men enjoy under our heritage of common law long antedate the sixteenth century. But they do not. The Magna Charta, for example, could not be invoked in cases of treason, or sedition. Only loyal subjects of the crown could claim its benefits. The mere accusation of a treasonable act barred the defendent from those protections devised for the trial of less heinous crimes such as murder. There were, accordingly, strong incentives for the use of cryptic writing in the age of Shakespeare. In times when jury men were jailed for their acquital of an accused traitor, as Throckmorton's jury was, men had to resort to subterfuge to express their deepest convictions. Although seditious works such as *The Isle of Dogs* and the *Martin Marprelate* pamphlets could be so completely suppressed that not a single page of the one survives—and

4. *Studies in the Book of Lamentations* (1954), Ch. 1, N. K. GOTTWALD

very little of the other—the driven men who wrote them found other avenues of release for the pressures which motivated them. Censorship as a tool of tyranny can never be completely successful. Could the Shakespearean works have been published under a burden of censorship?

Possibly the author, master genius that he was, could have delved more deeply into acrostic composition than others of his time as a means of outflanking his censors. That he did just this will hereafter be shown by uncovering a series of acrostic patterns, in the original Shakespeare texts, which by their astounding ingenuity, their wide extent and their frequent waggish jests seem almost beyond the capacity of the human mind to execute. The Friedmans, despite their disparagement of the Shakespearean ciphers, do view acrostics as a possibility.

"We should not be surprised if it is claimed that anagrams or acrostics appear in Shakespeare's works, for they abounded in the literature of the time; nor should we be surprised if these devices concern the authorship of the works, for they have often been used to this end. We should even be tolerant of variable and erratic spelling, for this was to some extent a common Elizabethan practice. The only thing we need insist on is that the systems used should satisfy the conditions for validity . . ." p. 101

The Friedmans have also laid down certain standards which must be met if a purported acrostic is to be recognized as intentional. In must consistently follow a single system. The hidden message must make sense throughout, and the length of the message or the extent of its repetition must be so great that it could not have occured fortuitously. Also, the cryptic message must be derivable by different individuals working independently.

Acrostic patterns intended by an author will, of course, not survive re-editing and reprinting such as the Shakespeare works have undergone. We must go to the original first editions, all of which are fortunately available in fascimile. But here we encounter strange type faces and even stranger spelling. The letter *s* looks like *f,* the *v* is used for *u* and vice-versa and we find *i* being used in place of *j* as well as of *y.* On top of this, the spelling is atrociously casual. But if these impediments can be overcome there is more acrostic gold to be found in Shakespeare than Raleigh and Drake together brought in from the Spanish Main. The following pages will be devoted to an exploration of these acrostics, dwelling but briefly on their significance and their effect on the recorded history of the time; which is a study in itself.

According to a theory first propounded in 1920,[5] the Shakespeare plays, the poems, and the Sonnets are the work of Edward de Vere, the 17th Earl of Oxford. The genius which so fluently expressed the entire range of human emotion and motivation and which is revered today the world over, lived in his breast. But he, for reasons which can be only surmised, adopted the pseudonym "William Shakespeare." No nobleman in those days would think of stooping to write poetry for publication. Those who were poetically inclined would only put their brain children in manuscript form and circulate them among their aristocratic friends. These were often copied and recopied but never printed, at least until after the author had passed away.

Although we readily accept the fact of an assumed name for such authors as Mark Twain (Samuel Clemens), George Eliot (Marian Evans) and Lewis Carroll (Charles L. Dodgson), somehow the idea that William Shakespeare could be a pen name falls into a different category. The reason, of course, is that there did live from 1564 to 1616 a flesh and blood man by that name, or a very similar one. There exist today records of his baptism, marriage, and death at Stratford-on-Avon and a meagre scattering of other documents flowing from some of his activities there and at London.

5. *Shakespeare Identified,* J. Thomas Looney

Included are six examples of his signature, and these brief scrawls constitute everything that has been found of his handwriting.

Edward de Vere belonged to the nobility and as such was set apart from the common folk. It was beneath his station to write or produce plays, which was the province of mountebanks and riff-raff of the lowest sort. But de Vere could avoid this stigma and still find outlet for his creative pressures by adopting a pseudonym. He chose the name William Shakespeare. Consequently, the writings that have come down to us under his real name are quite meagre and belong excusively to his very early years. As the Shakespeare name became more familiar to the public who attended and admired the dramas, it probably also became evident that the author himself was nowhere in evidence and wished to remain, or perhaps was forced to remain, in obscurity.

When the flesh and blood Shakespeare came to London and learned of this, the confusion between the two Shakespears began. The man of Stratford by the coincidence of his similar name allowed himself to be passed off as the popular author and was made the butt of an immense practical joke by the gay blades of the London theatre set. Just as *A Lord* and his friends in the induction to *The Taming of the Shrew* make sport with the ignorant and uncouth *Sly* so the Stratford "Shaxper" was led on into believing that he had become a gentleman and would be acknowledged as the popular playwright of the same name. The story was later developed in Ben Johnson's allegory "Every Man Out of his Humor" where *Sogliardo*—The Stratford Man—was unmercifully duped by the friends of *Puntarvolo*—Lord Oxford—into personating the playwrite before the Queen. Eventually, the Stratford man confused the ruse with the facts too frequently and the interloper had to be paid off to go back to Stratford, where he became the owner of the finest house in town. He was paid the then extravagent sum of £1,000 by the Earl of Southhampton, the unacknowledged natural son of Lord Oxford.

De Vere, by historical record, was the premier Earl of England and Lord Great Chamberlain. He was brought up as a Royal Ward from the age of twelve and educated in the arts and sports of the nobility. His tutor was Arthur Golding, who translated Ovid's *Metamorphoses* from which so many classical allusions in Shakespeare are drawn. He learned the law at the Inns of Court and traveled on the Continent, particularly in Italy. De Vere as a young man wrote a number of poems over his own name. He was a court figure at an early age and at twenty-two produced, in collaboration with Sir Fulke Greville, a mock battle for the court which was on a "progress" at Warwick Castle. It was so realistic that the producers had to rescue the residents of a nearby house ignited by the fireworks. De Vere, Greville and Sir Phillip Sidney were close friends as young men and shared strong interests and talents in letters. Today the secluded room in Warwick Castle which was Greville's study displays three large portraits in matching size and style of Greville, Sidney and "Shakespeare." After Lord Oxford's death, his widow sold their last residence, King's Place in Hackney, to Sir Fulke, by then Lord Brooke.

Reverting to the theory, de Vere became a brilliant ornament of Elizabeth's court and wrote and staged the entertainments for the Revels. These were the Shakespeare plays in their early forms and were produced only for court amusement. As such, they were filled with topical allusions and probably revised from year to year to bring in references to later events and jibes at different personalities. Later the company of players was allowed to present versions for public audinces, first at inns and later at structures especially built for presenting plays. De Vere became absorbed in dramatic production and dissipated his fortune in supporting players and writers. In the process he became quite Bohemian and eventually fell from Elizabeth's favor. It is known that he was imprisoned in the Tower for a few weeks and at another time was banished from court. He probably fell into some deeper disgrace in middle age as many of the Sonnets testify.

The last decade or two of his life was spent in retirement, after his first wife died and he had married Elizabeth Trentham, a wealthy and beautiful former lady-in-waiting. Dur-

14

ing these years he rewrote his plays, transforming them from mere stage pieces to the great literature we have today. The poems and Sonnets are of this period also. This was long after the Stratford man had been sent back to the country but, nevertheless, almost the entire work of this giant of literature came to us in print under the name of William Shakespeare.

The reasons for such a monstrous travesty upon posterity must have been weighty indeed. Would not the real identity of so great a genius break through the most rigorous censorship, at least by the time the figures concerned had passed on? Either something very disgraceful or some matters of vital importance to the state must have been involved.

The facts will never be capable of proof, but there is now solid support for the theory that Lord Oxford was forced to remain unidentified with the plays of "Shakespeare" in order to preserve the state secret that he had been the Queen's lover and that there was a child of the union, who was Henry Wriothesley, the Earl of Southhampton. The previous evidence has been extensive but entirely circumstantial and deductive.[6] What is about to appear is the direct evidence in the Bard's very own words, that ties Edward de Vere to the works and to the pseudonym William Shakespeare. The interesting corollary moreover is the amazing degree to which his talent with words extended. This genius was a genius far greater than anyone has recognized or even conceived possible. He was a master word weaver not only in our accustomed forms of poetry and drama but at the same time he produced visual patterns of acrostics of unbelievable complexity.

An example of one of his simpler visual patterns is shown on the following page. These are facsimiles of portions of Sonnets 37 through 42 taken from the first edition (1609) of *SHAKE-SPEARES SONNETS*. Outlined by

6. See *This Star of England*, Ch. 61. Dorothy & Charlton Ogburn, New York 1952

chains of circles are certain acrostically alined letters which spell the name VERE—with variant spellings. These are so located in the text that—much like toothpicks laid out on a table—they form certain large letters. These large letters are so placed, one in each Sonnet, as to spell the name OXFORD, as indicated by the broad colored outlines.

But this is getting ahead of the story.

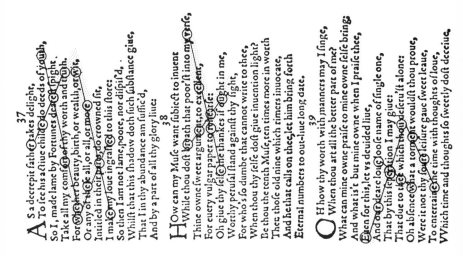

HHH

CHAPTER 2

SOME ANSWERS DISCOVERED

The name "Vere" is the acrostic which is found more than two thousand times in the Shakespeare works. At first the author used it merely as a hidden signature at the beginning and at the end of a piece. It can be spelled two ways, "Vere" or Veer." It can also be formed with the letter *u* instead of *v*—and these letters are used interchangeably throughout the literature of the time. One farther step gave him added latitude, namely, the letter *w* could represent the *v* since it is a double *v* in appearance, although a double *u* by

name.—Incidentally, where would *W* have acquired its name
if *V* and *U* were not the same letter in the early days?—He
thus had available six different ways to form an acrostic
signature—Vere, Veer, Uere, Ueer, Were, and Weer. He
made use of all of them.

The first publication ever to carry the by-line "William
Shakespeare" was the poem "Venus and Adonis" printed in
1593. This was probably a trial balloon to see whether his
acrostic signature would be recognized by the Queen and the
"establishment" which had muzzled him.

VENVS AND ADONIS.

E V E N as the funne with purple-colourd face,
Had tane his laft leaue of the weeping morne,
Rofe-cheekt Adonis hied him to the chace,
Hunting he lou'd, but loue he laught to fcorne :
Sick-thoughted Venus makes amaine vnto him,
And like a bold fac'd futer ginnes to woo him,

Thrife fairer then my felfe, (thus fhe began)

Here is "Ueer" running right across the first four lines in
the middle. Here also is a key that signals its location; and
this key has been used with faithful consistency throughout.
In the margin is found an acrostic word—any word at all—
except that it has some meaningful association with the adjacent text. Here the "signal" is the word "SAT" in the margin of lines five to seven. It "links" in meaning to the words
"makes amaine," an archaic expression for the lowering of
a ship's sails and figuratively the act of a lady in spreading
her skirts to sit down on the ground, as Venus does in the
poem. This pattern of a marginal acrostic word as a "signal,"
a "link" in the adjacent text, and a Vere acrostic buried in
the body of the text is the foundation system for all that
follows.

18

Occasionally the signal word will be Latin or Greek. This gives a more vital significance to Ben Jonson's famous lines "And though thou hadst small Latin and lesse Greek from thence to honour thee I would not seek for names" (Vere's). Jonson is saying, in the full context, that if he could speak across the years instead of to his own dangerous times he wouldn't have to rely on these acrostics to show the true identity of his beloved Shakespeare but he would "call forth thundering" his name. Jonson was aware of the acrostic system because he used it in his introductory pieces for the first folio edition of the plays. For example, here is the famous piece located across the page from the engraved head of Shakespeare.

To the Reader.

This Figure, that thou here seeſt put,
    It vvas for gentle Shakeſpeare cut;
Wherein the Grauer had a ſtrife
    with Nature, to out-doo the life :
O, could he but haue dravvne his vvit
    As vvell in braſſe, as he hath hit.
His face ; the Print vvould then ſurpaſſe
    All, that vvas euer vvrit in braſſe.
But, ſince he cannot, Reader, looke
    Not on his Picture, but his Booke.

B. I.

Note that the acrostic extends over five lines and reads both up and down.

Returning to "Venus and Adonis" here is the last stanza.

Thus weary of the world, away fhe hies,
And yokes her filuer doues, by whofe fwift aide,
Their miftreffe mounted through the emptie skies,
In her light chariot, quickly is conuaide,
  Holding their courfe to Paphos, where their queen,
  Meanes to immure her felfe, and not be feen.
FINIS

The signal is "HIT," which links to "swift' in the second line. The signature, which will be called the "namestick" hereafter, is found only by using "er" from the last line, which is hardly legitimate. But he verifies its legitimacy here by an immediate repetition in line 2 of the stanza. The namestick is thus six lines long and comprises two "Vere's."

If all this has an air of fantasy about it, it is because it was done with great caution in fear of imprisonment, torture and death. No doubt the use of a link to the text served a dual purpose. Besides confirming the intentional nature of the marginal signal to the informed ultimate reader, it gave an innocent excuse for its presence in case the inquisitioners wanted to know about it. However that may be, we don't have to wait long for a clearer demonstration of the system. After a year had passed without the device being detected in the wrong quarters he published a second poem, again on the subject of illicit lust but this time instead of the woman, the man was the aggressor. Perhaps the Queen, who was seventeen years older than de Vere and merely bcause of rank would have needed to take the initiative in any love affair with him, resented the implications of the first poem. Here are the first and last stanzas of "The Rape of Lucrece" which show the same system used in easily recognizable form.

From the besieged Ardea all in post,
Borne by the trustlesse wings of false desire,
Lust-breathed Tarqvin, leaues the Roman host,
And to Colatium beares the lightlesse fire,
VVhich in pale embers hid, lurkes to aspire,
  And girdle with embracing flames, the wast
Of Colatine fair loue, Lvcrece the chast.

VVhen they had sworne to this aduised doome,
They did conclude to beare dead Lvcrece thence,
To shew her bleeding bodie thorough Roome,
And so to publish Tarqvins fowle offence;
VVhich being done, with speedie diligence,
  The Romaines plausibly did giue consent,
To Tarqvins euerlasting banishment.

N

F I N I S.

"Tuat" is Latin for "he shows," linking to "Shew" in the fifth last line. It should not be necessary to display here the similar signals, links, and namesticks which occur in the dedication pages for each of the poems. They, incidentally, were dedicated in endearing personal terms to the Earl of Southhampton, by then a young man.

The pattern of signing each piece at the beginning and end continues in the plays. Here are the relevant lines and namesticks from the four best known stage speeches in all the world.

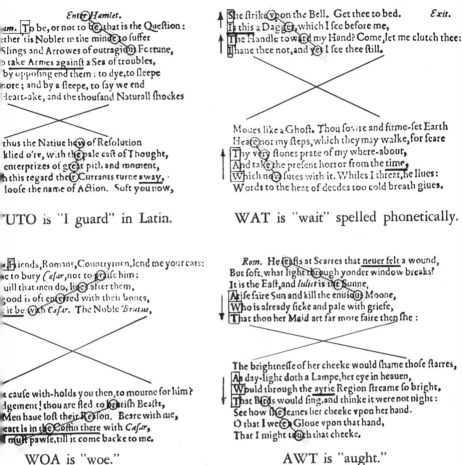

The reader will have noticed that the marginal signals and links are sometimes strained. If a word is spelled phonetically in the margin, many would dismiss it as accidental. Those who would may do so—but they will miss some touches of sly whimsy. As more and more of these are encountered the intentional nature of the signals begins to appear. There are several, such as WAT for WAIT and STA for STAY, which occur at places where the author needs to warn the reader that something important is about to show up. This and other devices appear often enough to make it reasonably certain that the short phonetic signals which have a link to the text are intentional. For example, he calls attention to his more elaborate namestick patterns with the signal WIT in a score of places.

Perhaps the most challenging and at the same time amusing aspects lies in the witty ways in which he links the text to the signal. This is often a test of the reader's ingenuity very comparable to the obscurities used in some cross-word puzzle definitions. Unlike the cross-word puzzles, however, temptation toward outright bawdy connotations is not always held in check. Oxford and his father-in-law, Lord Burleigh, bickered frequently over Oxford's "lewd friends."

Without giving any more examples from the plays, it is clear that a confirmed pattern of start and finish namesticks exists. This book will not undertake the task, but it can be shown that each play does carry a series of namesticks on both its first page and on its last page with many of the pages showing elaborate visual patterns.

Turning to the Sonnets, we find the outpourings of a tormented spirit. The man, whoever we may believe it was who wrote under that name, is almost universally recognized as having penned his most intimate thoughts in those 154 verses. The enigmas they present have baffled scholars and critics to this day. They disagree widely about the order in which they were written. Nor can the identity of the fair youth, the dark lady or the other personalities they concern be established with any approach to consensus.

The Sonnets present the most amazing display of acrostics. What's more, they are seen to develop progressively throughout the series. The author's skill at devising and executing these word tapestries grows increasingly, which for one thing, lays to rest all questions about the sequence in which the Sonnets were written.

The ensuing pages are facsimiles of the 154 Sonnets as first published. They are marked to show the signals, links, and namesticks, the signal appearing where the marginal letters have been marked with square outlines and an arrow showing whether to read up or down. The links are underlined in the text. The namesticks are indicated by chains of circles. Modern spellings of phonetic or archaic signals are shown in the left-hand margin while the right margin carries individual alphabetical letters added to those in the acrostics where advantageous. In creating these acrostics our author consistently followed certain self-imposed rules.

1. The namestick must be made up of letters which lie reasonably in alinement. A straight line must pass through some part at least of each one.

2. There must be at least four letters spelling Vere, de Vere, or occasionally E Ver. In a complex pattern there may be a short namestick Ver when necessary if the principal strokes of the pattern utilize four or more letters each.

3. Each namestick will utilize one letter, and only one, from each line which it crosses. No line is skipped unless the namestick lies clear of the end of a short line to pick up a letter near the end of a longer line. This rule has been stretched occasionally in some of the later Sonnets to allow a namestick to pass through the clear space between two words.

4. Each component stroke of a large letter is made with a separate namestick (or two). In the case of curved letters such as O or D, they are necessarily reduced to a pattern of four or five straight strokes.

5. The namestick may be too long, in which case the excess is ignored just as a toothpick would be broken off to the required length.

6. Where two component strokes meet or cross they may utilize either a common letter or separate ones. Occasionally a namestick will not quite reach a corner or otherwise fall a little short of its ideal terminus without being rejected, but it will always delineate a major portion of the component stroke.

7. Many of the patterns of four or more acrostics can be taken as more than one letter. For example, a pattern of four namesticks forming a square can be either an O or a D. The choice will obviously depend upon the preceding and following letters.

8. The large letters may lie tilted, upside down, or be a mirror image of the true letter. The system is naturally restricted in its capabilities because inherently there can be no horizontal namesticks.

9. There is a signal in the margin and a meaningful link in the text for every namestick, or for every large letter formed by a series of namesticks.

10. The signals are frequently spelled phonetically but the mental connection with the link is always present, though sometimes a bit esoteric.

11. The signals in the margin utilize a letter from each line which they span even though one or more lines may be indented.

12. A signal may read up or down and sometimes both ways.

13. The signals in the margin utilize the initial letters of the lines of speech, disregarding the speech ascriptions.

14. The internal acrostics or namesticks do occasionally utilize a speech ascription.

15. A small amount of poetic license can be exercised with any of these rules.

It is suggested that the reader proceed through the Sonnets in regular order for the fullest appreciation of the acrostics.

CHAPTER 3

SEARCHING THE SONNETS

SHAKE-SPEARES

SONNETS.

Neuer before Imprinted.

AT LONDON
By G. Eld for T. T. and are
to be folde by william Afley.
1609. Q 4

This namestick may not be intentional. It spans only three lines, and requires taking RE from a single line. However, note the signal BAN which links in meaning with "Neuer." This might be a defiant allusion to an imposed censorship.

TO . THE . ONLIE . BEGETTER . OF.

THESE . INSVING . SONNETS.

M#r#. W. H. ALL . HAPPINESSE.

AND . THAT . ETERNITIE.

PROMISED.

BY.

OVR . EVER-LIVING . POET.

WISHETH.

THE . WELL-WISHING.

ADVENTVRER . IN.

SETTING.

FORTH.

T. T.

Another imperfect namestick E (for Edward) VER, but again
a very evident signal SAT linking with SETTING. The vague,
obscure meaning of the last four lines is apparently due to the
demands of the acrostics. Whoever composed this and the title
page in G. Eld's print shop five years after de Vere's demise
was aware of the system but unable to apply it with comparable skill.

28

S H A K E-S P E A R E S,
SONNETS.

FRom faireſt creatures we deſire increaſe,
    That thereby beauties *Roſe* might neuer die,
But as the riper ſhould by time deceaſe,
His tender heire might beare his memory:
But thou contracted to thine owne bright eyes,
Feed'ſt thy lights flame with ſelfe ſubſtantiall fewell,
Making a famine where aboundance lies,
Thy ſelfe thy foe, to thy ſweet ſelfe too cruell:
Thou that art now the worlds freſh ornament,
And only herauld to the gaudy ſpring,
Within thine owne bud burieſt thy content,
And tender chorle makſt waſt in niggarding:
    Pitty the world, or elſe this glutton be,
    To eate the worlds due, by the graue and thee.

2

VVHen fortie Winters ſhall beſeige thy brow,
    And digge deep trenches in thy beauties field,
Thy youthes proud liuery ſo gaz'd on now,
Wil be a totter'd weed of ſmal worth held:
Then being askt, where all thy beautie lies,
Where all the treaſure of thy luſty daies;
To ſay within thine owne deepe ſunken eyes,
Were an all-eating ſhame, and thriftleſſe praiſe.
How much more praiſe deſeru'd thy beauties vſe,
If thou couldſt anſwere this faire child of mine
Shall ſum my count, and make my old excuſe
Proouing his beautie by ſucceſſion thine.

B   This

The author has confirmed the intentional nature of WAT for
WAIT by repeating it immediately. Also he has chosen a word
which tells the reader to pause and look for more than meets
the eye. Sonnet 1 has merely a signature at start and finish but
sonnet 2 begins a more complex pattern. Here the four namesticks are arranged to form a large "W.'

S HAKE-SPEARES,

SONNETS.

FRom faireſt creatures we deſire increaſe,
That thereby beauties *Roſe* might neuer die,
But as the riper ſhould by time deceaſe,
His tender heire might beare his memory :
But thou contracted to thine owne bright eyes,
Feed'ſt thy lights flame with ſelfe ſubſtantiall fewell,
Making a famine where aboundance lies,
Thy ſelfe thy foe, to thy ſweet ſelfe too cruell :
Thou that art now the worlds freſh ornament,
And only herauld to the gaudy ſpring,
Within thine own bud burieſt thy content,
And tender chorle makſt waſt in niggarding :
    Pitty the world, or elſe this glutton be,
    To eate the worlds due, by the graue and thee.

2

VVHen fortie Winters ſhall beſeige thy brow,
And digge deep trenches in thy beauties field,
Thy youthes proud liuery ſo gaz'd on now,
Wil be a totter'd weed of ſmal worth held :
Then being askt, where all thy beautie lies,
Where all the treaſure of thy luſty daies ;
To ſay within thine owne deepe ſunken eyes,
Where an all-eating ſhame, and thriftleſſe praiſe.
How much more praiſe deſeru'd thy beauties vſe,
If thou couldſt anſwere this faire child of mine
Shall ſum my count, and make my old excuſe
Proouing his beautie by ſucceſſion thine.

       B   This

SHAKE-SPEARES

This were to be new made when thou art ould,
And fee thy blood warme when thou feel'ft it could,

3

Looke in thy glaffe and tell the face thou vewest,
Now is the time that face fhould forme an other,
Whofe frefh repaire if now thou not reneweft,
Thou doo'ft beguile the world, vnbleffe fome mother.
For where is fhe fo faire whofe vn-eard wombe
Difdaines the tillage of thy husbandry?
Or who is he fo fond will be the tombe,
Of his felfe loue to ftop pofterity?
Thou art thy mothers glaffe and fhe in thee
Calls backe the louely Aprill of her prime,
So thou through windowes of thine age fhalt fee,
Difpight of wrinkles this thy goulden time.
But if thou liue remembred not to be,
Die fingle and thine Image dies with thee.

TUNE

I

L

4

Vnthrifty louelineffe why doft thou fpend,
Vpon thy felfe thy beauties legacy?
Natures bequeft giues nothing but doth lend,
And being franck fhe lends to thofe are free:
Then beautious nigard why dooft thou abufe,
The bountious largeffe giuen thee to giue?
Profitles vferer why dooft thou vfe
So great a fumme of fummes yet can'ft not liue?
For hauing traffike with thy felfe alone,
Thou of thy felfe thy fweet felfe doft deceaue,
Then how when nature calls thee to be gone,
What acceptable *Audit* can'ft thou leaue?
Thy vnuf'd beauty muft be tomb'd with thee,
Which vfed liues th'executor to be.

TA'EN

L

5

Thofe howers that with gentle worke did frame,
The louely gaze where euery eye doth dwell
Will play the tirants to the very fame,

And

Two marginal signals indicate that two letter formations are to be found in sonnet 3.

This were to be new made when thou art ould,
And ſee thy blood warme when thou feel'ſt it could,

3

LOoke in thy glaſſe and tell the face thou veweſt,
Now is the time that face ſhould forme an other,
Whoſe freſh repaire if now thou not reneweſt,
Thou doo'ſt beguile the world, vnbleſſe ſome mother.
For where is ſhe ſo faire whoſe vn-eard wombe
Diſdaines the tillage of thy husbandry?
Or who is he ſo fonde will be the tombe,
Of his ſelfe loue to ſtop poſterity?
Thou art thy mothers glaſſe and ſhe in thee
Calls backe the louely Aprill of her prime,
So thou through windowes of thine age ſhalt ſee,
Diſpight of wrinkles this thy goulden time.
  But if thou liue remembred not to be,
  Die ſingle and thine Image dies with thee.

4

VNthrifty louelineſſe why doſt thou ſpend,
Vpon thy ſelfe thy beauties legacy?
Natures bequeſt giues nothing but doth lend,
And being franck ſhe lends to thoſe are free :
Then beautious nigard why dooſt thou abuſe,
The bountious largeſſe giuen thee to giue?
Profitles vſerer why dooſt thou vſe
So great a ſumme of ſummes yet can'ſt not liue?
For hauing traffike with thy ſelfe alone,
Thou of thy ſelfe thy ſweet ſelfe doſt deceaue,
Then how when nature calls thee to be gone,
What acceptable *Audit* can'ſt thou leaue?
  Thy vnuſ'd beauty muſt be tomb'd with thee,
  Which vſed liues th' executor to be.

5

THoſe howers that with gentle worke did frame,
The louely gaze where euery eye doth dwell
Will play the tirants to the very ſame,

And

32

SONNETS.

And that vnfaire which fairely doth excell:
For neuer resting time leads Summer on,
To hidious winter and confounds him there,
Sap checkt with frost and lustie leau's quite gon,
Beauty ore-snow'd and barenes euery where,
Then were not summers distillation left
A liquid prisoner pent in walls of glasse,
Beauties effect with beauty were bereft,
Nor it nor noe remembrance what it was.
But flowers distil'd though they with winter meete,
Leese but their show,their substance still liues sweet.

I
A

BAIT

6

THen let not winters wragged hand deface,
In thee thy summer ere thou be distil'd:
Make sweet some viall;treasure thou some place,
With beautits treasure ere it be selfe kil'd:
That vse is not forbidden vsery,
Which happies those that pay the willing lone;
That's for thy selfe to breed an other thee,
Or ten times happier be it ten for one,
Ten times thy selfe were happier then thou art,
If ten of thine ten times refigur'd thee,
Then what could death doe if thou should'st depart,
Leauing thee liuing in posterity?
Be not selfe-wild for thou art much too faire,
To be deaths conquest and make wormes thine heire.

M

TOTE

7

LOe in the Orient when the gracious light,
Lifts vp his burning head,each vnder eye
Doth homage to his new appearing sight,
Seruing with lookes his sacred maiesty,
And hauing climb'd the steepe vp heauenly hill,
Resembling strong youth in his middle age,
Yet mortall lookes adore his beauty still,
Attending on his goulden pilgrimage:
But when from high-most pich with wery car,

AIR

B 2   Lik-

Sonnets 5 and 6 show patterns of namesticks forming three
more letters so that, reading from sonnet 2, the name W I L-
L I A M is spelled out

And that vnfaire which fairely doth excell :
For neuer refting time leads Summer on,
To hidious winter and confounds him there,
Sap checkt with froft and luftie leau's quite gon.
Beauty ore-fnow'd and barenes euery where,
Then were not fummers diftillation left
A liquid prifoner pent in walls of glaffe,
Beauties effect with beauty were bereft,
Nor it nor noe remembrance what it was.
   But flowers diftil'd though they with winter meete,
   Leefe but their fhow, their fubftance ftill liues fweet.

6

THen let not winter's wragged hand deface,
   In thee thy fummer ere thou be diftil'd :
Make fweet fome viall ; treafure thou fome place,
With beautits treafure ere it be felfe kil'd :
That vfe is not forbidden vfery,
Which happies thofe that pay the willing lone ;
That's for thy felfe to breed an other thee,
Or ten times happier be it ten for one,
Ten times thy felfe were happier then thou art,
If ten of thine ten times refigur'd thee,
Then what could death doe if thou fhould'ft depart,
Leauing thee liuing in pofterity?
   Be not felfe-wild for thou art much too faire,
   To be deaths conqueft and make wormes thine heire.

7

LOe in the Orient when the gracious light.
   Lifts vp his burning head, each vnder eye
Doth homage to his new appearing fight,
Seruing with lookes his facred maiefty,
And hauing climb'd the fteepe vp heauenly hill,
Refembling ftrong youth in his middle age,
Yet mortall lookes adore his beauty ftill,
Attending on his goulden pilgrimage :
But when from high-moft pich with wery car,
          B 2   Like

SHAKE-SPEARES

Like feeble age he reeleth from the day,
The eyes(fore dutious)now conuerted are
From his low tract and looke an other way:
  So thou,thy selfe out-going in thy noon:
  Vnlok'd on diest vnlesse thou get a sonne.

8

MVsick to heare,why hear'st thou musick sadly,
  Sweets with sweets warre not , ioy delights in ioy:
Why lou'st thou that which thou receaust not gladly,
Or else receau'st with pleasure thine annoy ?
If the true concord of well tuned sounds,
By vnions married do offend thine eare,
They do but sweetly chide thee, who confounds
In singlenesse the parts that thou should'st beare:
Marke how one string sweet husband to an other,
Strikes each in each by mutuall ordering;
Resembling sier,and child, and happy mother,
Who all in one,one pleasing note do sing:
  Whose speechlesse song being many,seeming one,
  Sings this to thee thou single wilt proue none.

9.

IS it for feare to wet a widdowes eye,
  That thou consum'st thy selfe in single life?
Ah;if thou issulesse shalt hap to die,
The world will waile thee like a makelesse wife,
The world wilbe thy widdow and still weepe,
That thou no forme of thee hast left behind,
When euery priuat widdow well may keepe,
By childrens eyes,her husbands shape in minde:
Looke what an vnthrift in the world doth spend
Shifts but his place,for still the world inioyes it
But beauties waste hath in the world an end,
And kept vnvsde the vser so destroyes it:
  No loue toward others in that bosome sits
  That on himselfe such murdrous shame commits.

10.

will I

TIME

S

H

With the two letters S and H formed in Sonnets 8 and 9 it
may be guessed what is coming. Notice that the signal BAN is
repeated and will be again.

Like feeble age he reeleth from the day,
The eyes (fore dutious) now conuerted are
From his low tract and looke an other way :
  So thou, thy felfe out-going in thy noon :
  Vnlok'd on dieft vnleffe thou get a fonne.

8

MVfick to heare, why hear'ft thou mufick fadly,
  Sweets with fweets warre not, ioy delights in ioy :
Why lou'ft thou that which thou receauft not gladly,
Or elfe receau'ft with pleafure thine annoy ?
If the true concord of well tuned founds,
By vnions married do offend thine eare,
They do but fweetly chide thee, who confounds
In finglenetfe the parts that thou fhould'ft beare :
Marke how one ftring fweet husband to an other,
Strikes each in each by mutuall ordering ;
Refembling fier, and child, and happy mother,
Who all in one, one pleafing note do fing :
  Whofe fpeechleffe fong being many, feeming one,
  Sings this to thee thou fingle wilt proue none.

9.

IS it for feare to wet a widdowes eye,
  That thou confum'ft thy felfe in fingle life ?
Ah ; if thou iffuleffe fhalt hap to die,
The world will waile thee like a makeleffe wife,
The world wilbe thy widdow and ftill weepe,
That thou no forme of thee haft left behind,
When euery priuat widdow well may keepe,
By childrens eyes, her husbands fhape in minde :
Looke what an vnthrift in the world doth fpend
Shifts but his place, for ftill the world inioyes it
But beauties wafte hath in the world an end,
And kept vnvfde the vfer fo deftroyes it :
  No loue toward others in that bofome fits
  That on himfelfe fuch murdrous fhame commits.

IO.

SONNETS.

10

FOr shame deny that thou bear'st loue to any
Who for thy selfe art so vnprouident
Graunt if thou wilt, thou art belou'd of many,
But that thou none lou'st is most euident:
For thou art so possest with murdrous hate,
That gainst thy selfe thou stickst not to conspire,
Seeking that beautious roofe to ruinate
Which to repaire should be thy chiefe desire:
O change thy thought, that I may change my minde,
Shall hate be fairer log'd then gentle loue?
Be as thy presence is gracious and kind,
Or to thy selfe at least kind harted proue,
    Make thee an other selfe for loue of me,
    That beauty still may liue in thine or thee.

11

AS fast as thou shalt wane so fast thou grow'st,
In one of thine, from that which thou departest,
And that fresh bloud which yongly thou bestow'st,
Thou maist call thine, when thou from youth conuertest,
Herein liues wisdome, beauty, and increase,
Without this follie, age, and could decay,
If all were minded so, the times should cease,
And threescoore yeare would make the world away:
Let those whom nature hath not made for store,
Harsh, featurelesse, and rude, barrenly perrish,
Looke whom she best indow'd, she gaue the more;
Which bountious guift thou shouldst in bounty cherrish,
    She caru'd thee for her seale, and ment therby,
    Thou shouldst print more, not let that coppy die.

12

VVHen I doe count the clock that tels the time,
And see the braue day sunck in hidious night,
When I behold the violet past prime,
And sable curls or siluer'd ore with white:
When lofty trees I see barren of leaues,
Which erst from heat did canopie the herd

B3   And

A deliberate typographical error is introduced here to produce
the namestick—a clear indication of intent rather than accident.
Sonnet 12 in line 4 has "or silvered ore" instead of "all silvered
ore" so that the r in "ore" will fall into alignment.

10

FOr fhame deny that thou bear'ft loue to any
Who for thy felfe art fo vnprouident
Graunt if thou wilt, thou art belou'd of many,
But that thou none lou'ft is moft euident :
For thou art fo poffeft with murdrous hate,
That gainft thy felfe thou ftickft not to confpire,
Seeking that beautious roofe to ruinate
Which to repaire fhould be thy chiefe defire :
O change thy thought, that I may change my minde,
Shall hate be fairer log'd then gentle loue ?
Be as thy prefence is gracious and kind,
Or to thy felfe at leaft kind harted proue,
    Make thee an other felfe for loue of me,
    That beauty ftill may liue in thine or thee.

11

AS faft as thou fhalt wane fo faft thou grow'ft,
In one of thine, from that which thou departeft,
And that frefh bloud which yongly thou beftow'ft,
Thou maift call thine, when thou from youth conuertest,
Herein liues wifdome, beauty, and increafe,
Without this follie, age, and could decay,
If all were minded fo, the times fhould ceafe,
And threefcoore yeare would make the world away :
Let thofe whom nature hath not made for ftore,
Harfh, featureleffe, and rude, barrenly perrifh,
Looke whom fhe beft indow'd, fhe gaue the more ;
Which bountious guift thou fhouldft in bounty cherrifh,
    She caru'd thee for her feale, and ment therby,
    Thou fhouldft print more, not let that coppy die.

12

WHen I doe count the clock that tels the time,
And fee the braue day funck in hidious night,
When I behold the violet paft prime,
And fable curls or filuer'd ore with white :
When lofty trees I fee barren of leaues,
Which erft from heat did canopie the herd
                    B 3   And

And Sommers greene all girded vp in sheaues
Borne on the beare with white and bristly beard:
Then of thy beauty do I question make
That thou among the wastes of time must goe,
Since sweets and beauties do them-selues forsake,
And die as fast as they see others grow,
And nothing gainst Times sieth can make defence
Saue breed to braue him,when he takes thee hence.

SAY

13

O That you were your selfe,but loue you are
No longer yours,then you your selfe here liue,
Against this cumming end you should prepare,
And your sweet semblance to some other giue.
So should that beauty which you hold in lease
Find no determination,then you were
You selfe again after your selfes decease,
When your sweet issue your sweet forme should beare.
Who lets so faire a house fall to decay,
Which husbandry in honour might vphold,
Against the stormy gusts of winters day
And barren rage of deaths eternall cold?
    O none but vnthrifts,deare my loue you know,
    You had a Father,let your Son say so.

WIFE

E

14

Not from the stars do I my iudgement plucke,
And yet me thinkes I haue Astronomy,
But not to tell of good,or euil lucke,
Of plagues,of dearths,or seasons quallity,
Nor can I fortune to breefe mynuits tell;
Pointing to each his thunder,raine and winde,
Or say with Princes if it shal go wel
By oft predict that I in heauen finde.
But from thine eies my knowledge I deriue,
And constant stars in them I read such art
As truth and beautie shal together thriue
If from thy selfe,to store thou wouldst conuert;

BAN

S

With BAN appearing now for the third time in eight pages we
may legitimately suspect the author of trying to register the
point that the true story was banned.

And Sommers greene all girded vp in fheaues
Borne on the beare with white and briftly beard :
Then of thy beauty do I queftion make
That thou among the waftes of time muft goe,
Since fweets and beauties do them-felues forsake,
And die as faft as they fee others grow,
    And nothing gainft Times fieth can make defence
    Saue breed to braue him, when he takes thee hence.

13

O That you were your felfe, but loue you are
  No longer yours, then you your felfe here liue,
Againft this cumming end you fhould prepare,
And your sweet femblance to fome other giue.
So fhould that beauty which you hold in leafe
Find no determination, then you were
You felfe again after your felfes deceafe,
When your fweet iffue your fweet forme ftould beare.
Who lets fo faire a houfe fall to decay,
Which husbandry in honour might vphold,
Againft the ftormy gufts of winters day
And barren rage of deaths eternall cold ?
    O none but vnthrifts, deare my loue you know,
    You had a Father, let your Son fay fo.

14

NOt from the ftars do I my judgement plucke,
  And yet me thinkes I haue Aftronomy,
But not to tell of good, or euil lucke,
Of plagues, of dearths, or feafons quallity,
Nor can I fortune to breefe mynuits tell ;
Pointing to each his thunder, raine and winde,
Or fay with Princes if it fhal go wel
By oft predict that I in heauen finde.
But from thine eies my knowledge I deriue,
And conftant ftars in them I read fuch art
As truth and beautie fhal together thriue
If from thy felfe, to ftore thou wouldft conuert :
                              Or

SONNETS.

Or elfe of thee this I prognofticate,
Thy end is Truthes and Beauties doome and date.

15

WHen I confider euery thing that growes
Holds in perfection but a little moment.
That this huge ftage prefenteth nought but fhowes
Whereon the Stars in fecret influence comment.
When I perceiue that men as plants increafe,
Cheared and checkt euen by the felfe-fame skie:
Vaunt in their youthfull fap, at height decreafe,
And were their braue ftate out of memory.
Then the conceit of this inconftant ftay,
Sets you moft rich in youth before my fight,
Where waftfull time debateth with decay
To change your day of youth to fullied night,
    And all in war with Time for loue of you
    As he takes from you, I ingraft you new.

STAY

16

BVt wherefore do not you a mightier waie
Make warre vppon this bloudie tirant time? ¡
And fortifie your felfe in your decay
With meanes more bleffed then my barren rime?
Now ftand you on the top of happie houres,
And many maiden gardens yet vnfet,
With vertuous wifh would beare your liuing flowers,
Much liker then your painted counterfeit:
So fhould the lines of life that life repaire
Which this (Times penfel or my pupill pen)
Neither in inward worth nor outward faire
Can make you liue your felfe in eies of men,
    To giue away your felfe, keeps your felfe ftill,
    And you muft liue drawne by your owne fweet skill,

WANE

17

VVHo will beleeue my verfe in time to come
If it were fild with your moft high deferts?
B 4   Though

STA occurs here for the first of five times in the Sonnets and at
least ten times in the plays. Most of the times it is found at a
place where it serves as a warning that an intricate acrostic
pattern is nearby.

Or elſe of thee this I prognoſticate,
Thy end is Truthes and Beauties doome and date.

15

WHen I consider euery thing that growes
Holds in perfeƈtion but a little moment.
That this huge ſtage preſenteth nought but ſhowes
Whereon the Stars in ſecret influence comment.
When I perceiue that men as plants increaſe,
Cheared and checkt euen by the ſelfe-ſame skie :
Vaunt in their youthfull ſap, at height decreaſe,
And were their braue ſtate out of memory.
Then the conceit of this inconſtant ſtay,
Sets you moſt rich in youth before my ſight,
Where waſtfull time debateth with decay
To change your day of youth to ſullied night,
    And all in war with Time for loue of you
    As he takes from you, I ingraft you new.

16

BVt wherefore do not you a mightier waie
Make warre vppon this bloudie tirant time?
And fortifie your ſelf in your decay
With means more bleſſed then my barren rime?
Now ſtand you on the top of happie houres,
And many maiden gardens yet vnſet,
With vertuous wiſh would beare your liuing flowers,
Much liker then your painted counterfeit :
So ſhould the lines of life that life repaire
Which this (Times penſel or my pupill pen)
Neither in inward worth nor outward faire
Can make you liue your ſelfe in eies of men,
    To giue away your ſelfe, keeps your ſelfe ſtill,
    And you muſt liue drawne by your owne ſweet skill,

17

WHo will beleeue my verſe in time to come
If it were ſild with your moſt high deſerts?
Though

SHAKE-SPEARES

Though yet heauen knowes it is but as a tombe
Which hides your life , and shewes not halfe your parts:
If I could write the beauty of your eyes,
And in fresh numbers number all your graces,
The age to come would say this Poet lies,
Such heauenly touches nere toucht earthly faces.
So should my papers (yellowed with their age)
Be scorn'd,like old men of lesse truth then tongue,
And your true rights be termd a Poets rage,
And stretched miter of an Antique song.
 But were some childe of yours aliue that time,
 You should liue twise in it,and in my rime.

18.

SHall I compare thee to a Summers day?
Thou art more louely and more temperate:
Rough windes do shake the darling buds of Maie,
And Sommers lease hath all too short a date:
Sometime too hot the eye of heauen shines,
And often is his gold complexion dimm'd,
And euery faire from faire some-time declines,
By chance,or natures changing course vntrim'd:
But thy eternall Sommer shall not fade,
Nor loose possession of that faire thou ow'st,
Nor shall death brag thou wandr'st in his shade,
When in eternall lines to time thou grow'st,
 So long as men can breath or eyes can see,
 So long liues this,and this giues life to thee,

19

DEuouring time blunt thou the Lyons pawes,
And make the earth deuoure her owne sweet brood,
Plucke the keene teeth from the fierce Tygers yawes,
And burne the long liu'd Phænix in her blood,
Make glad and sorry seasons as thou fleet'st,
And do what ere thou wilt swift-footed time
To the wide world and all her fading sweets:
But I forbid thee one most hainous crime,

O

STAY

BABY

SUN

PAD

A

With another STAI the author is inviting the reader to persist
since here he failed to place a letter formation in sonnets 17
and 18 but resumed the series in the 19th.

Though yet heauen knowes it is but as a tombe
Which hides your life, and fhewes not halfe your parts:
If I could write the beauty of your eyes,
And in frefh numbers number all your graces,
The age to come would fay this Poet lies,
Such heauenly touches nere toucht earthly faces.
So fhould my papers (yellowed with their age)
Be fcorn'd, like old men of leffe truth than tongue,
And your true rights be termed a Poets rage,
And ftretched miter of an Antique fong.
    But were fome childe of yours aliue that time,
    You fhould liue twife in it, and in my rime.

18.

SHall I compare thee to a Summers day?
  Thou art more louely and more temperate:
Rough windes do fhake the darling buds of Maie,
And Sommers leafe hath all too fhort a date:
Sometime too hot the eye of heauen fhines,
And often is his gold complexion dimm'd,
And euery faire from faire fome-time declines,
By chance, or natures changing courfe vntrim'd:
But thy eternall Sommer fhall not fade,
Nor loofe poffeffiion of that faire thou ow'ft,
Nor fhall death brag thou wandr'ft in his fhade,
When in eternall lines to time thou grow'ft,
    So long as men can breath or eyes can fee,
    So long liues this, and this giues life to thee,

19

DEuouring time blunt thou the Lyons pawes,
  And make the earth deuoure her own fweet brood,
Plucke the keene teeth from the fierce Tygers yawes,
And burne the long liu'd Phænix in her blood,
Make glad and forry feafons as thou fleet'ft,
And do what ere thou wilt fwift-footed time
To the wide world and all her fading fweets:
But I forbid thee one moft hainous crime,

                                   O

SONNETS.

O carue not with thy howers my loues faire brow,
Nor draw noe lines there with thine antique pen,
Him in thy courſe vntainted doe allow,
For beauties patterne to ſucceding men.
  Yet doe thy worſt ould Time diſpight thy wrong,
  My loue ſhall in my verſe euer liue young.

20

A Womans face with natures owne hand painted,
  Haſte thou the Maſter Miſtris of my paſſion,
A womans gentle hart but not acquainted
With ſhifting change as is falſe womens faſhion,
An eye more bright then theirs, leſſe falſe in rowling:
Gilding the obiect where-vpon it gazeth,
A man in hew all *Hews* in his controwling,
Which ſteales mens eyes and womens ſoules amaſeth.
And for a woman wert thou firſt created,
Till nature as ſhe wrought thee fell a dotinge,
And by addition me of thee defeated,
By adding one thing to my purpoſe nothing.
  But ſince ſhe prickt thee out for womens pleaſure,
  Mine be thy loue and thy loues vſe their treaſure.

21

S O is it not with me as with that Muſe,
  Stird by a painted beauty to his verſe,
Who heauen it ſelfe for ornament doth vſe,
And euery faire with his faire doth reherſe,
Making a coopelment of proud compare
With Sunne and Moone, with earth and ſeas rich gems:
With Aprills firſt borne flowers and all things rare,
That heauens ayre in this huge rondure hems,
O let me true in loue but truly write,
And then beleeue me, my loue is as faire,
As any mothers childe, though not ſo bright
As thoſe gould candells fixt in heauens ayer:
  Let them ſay more that like of heare-ſay well,
  I will not prayſe that purpoſe not to ſell.

C   22

The signal AWAT for AWAIT again invites us to carry on to
sonnet 21 for the next letter.

O carue not with thy howers my loues faire brow,
Nor draw noe lines there with thine antique pen.
Him in thy courfe vntainted doe allow,
For beauties patterne to fucceding men.
  Yet doe thy worft ould Time difpight thy wrong,
  My loue fhall in my verfe euer liue young.

20

A Womans face with natures owne hand painted,
  Hafte thou the Mafter Miftris of my paffion,
A womans gentle hart but not acquainted
With fhifting change as is falfe womens fafhion,
An eye more bright then theirs, leffe falfe in rowling :
Gilding the object where-vpon it gazeth,
A man in hew all *Hews* in his controwling,
Which fteales mens eyes and womens foules amafeth,
And for a woman wert thou first created,
Till nature as fhe wrought thee fell a dotinge,
And by addition me of thee defeated,
By adding one thing to my purpofe nothing.
  But fince fhe prickt thee out for womens pleafure,
  Mine be thy loue and thy loues vfe their treafure.

21

SO is it not with me as with that Mufe,
  Stird by a painted beauty to his verfe,
Who heauen it felfe for ornament doth vfe,
And euery faire with his faire doth reherfe,
Making a coopelment of proud compare
With Sunne and Moone, with earth and feas rich gems :
With Aprills firft borne flowers and all things rare,
That heauens ayre in this huge rondure hems,
O let me true in loue but truly write,
And then beleeue me, my loue is as faire,
As any mothers childe, though not fo bright
As thofe gould candells fixt in heauens ayer :
  Let them fay more that like of heare-fay well,
  I will not prayfe that purpofe not to fell.

C

22

22

MY glaffe fhall not perfwade me I am ould,
So long as youth and thou are of one date,
But when in thee times forrwes I behould,
Then look I death my daies fhould expiate.
For all that beauty that doth couer thee,
Is but the feemely rayment of my heart,
Which in thy breſt doth liue,as thine in me,
How can I then be elder then thou art?
O therefore loue be of thy felfe fo wary,
As I not for my felfe,but for thee will,
Bearing thy heart which I will keepe fo chary
As tender nurfe her babe from faring ill,
    Prefume not on thy heart when mine is flaine,
    Thou gau'ſt me thine not to giue backe againe.

WIFE

E

23

AS an vnperfect actor on the ſtage,
Who with his feare is put befides his part,
Or fome fierce thing repleat with too much rage,
Whofe ſtrengths abondance weakens his owne heart;
So I for feare of truſt,forget to fay,
The perfect ceremony of loues right,
And in mine owne loues ſtrength feeme to decay,
Ore-charg'd with burthen of mine owne loues might:
O let my books be then the eloquence,
And domb prefagers of my fpeaking breſt,
Who pleade for loue,and look for recompence,
More then that tonge that more hath more expreſt.
    O learne to read what filent loue hath writ,
    To heare wit eies belongs to loues fine wiht.

TOME WOE STAY VOW

AS

(SAY)

24

MIne eye hath play'd the painter and hath ſteeld,
Thy beauties forme in table of my heart,
My body is the frame wherein ti's held,
And perfpectiue it is beſt Painters art.
For through the Painter muſt you fee his skill,

To

With the E formed in Sonnett 22 the spelling of WILLIAM
SHAKESPEARE is complete.

Sonnet 23 tells how his love, the Queen, by her superior might
has silenced him, and so his books will be his unheard voice
if we but learn to read them. The namesticks are perfectly
arranged to spell SAIE (speak).

22

MY glaſſe ſhall not perſwade me I am ould,
So long as youth and thou are of one date,
But when in thee times forrwes I behould,
Then look I death my daies ſhould expiate.
For all that beauty that doth couer thee,
Is but the ſeemely rayment of my heart,
Which in thy breſt doth liue, as thine in me,
How can I then be elder then thou art ?
O therefore loue be of thy ſelfe ſo wary,
As I not for my ſelfe, but for thee will,
Bearing thy heart which I will keepe ſo chary
As tender nurſe her babe from faring ill,
    Preſume not on thy heart when mine is ſlaine,
    Thou gau'ſt me thine not to giue backe againe.

23

AS an vnperfect actor on the ſtage,
Who with his feare is put beſides his part,
Or ſome fierce thing repleat with too much rage,
Whoſe ſtrengths abondance weakens his owne heart ;
So I for feare of truſt, forget to ſay,
The perfect ceremony of loues right,
And in mine owne loues ſtrength ſeeme to decay,
Ore-charg'd with burthen of mine owne loues might :
O let my books be then the eloquence,
And domb preſagers of my ſpeaking breſt,
Who pleade for loue, and look for recompence,
More then that tonge that more hath more expreſt.
    O learne to read what ſilent loue hath writ,
    To heare wit eies belongs to loues fine wiht.

24

MIne eye hath play'd the painter and hath ſteeld,
Thy beauties forme in table of my heart,
My body is the frame wherein ti's held,
And perſpectiue it is beſt Painters art.
For through the Painter muſt you ſee his skill,

To

48

SONNETS.

To finde where your true Image pictur'd lies,
Which in my bofomes fhop is hanging ftil,
That hath his windowes glazed with thine eyes:
Now fee what good-turnes eyes for eies haue done,
Mine eyes haue drawne thy fhape, and thine for me
Are windowes to my breft, where-through the Sun
Delights to peepe, to gaze therein on thee
    Yet eyes this cunning want to grace their art
    They draw but what they fee, know not the hart.

2 5

LEt thofe who are in fauor with their ftars,
Of publike honour and proud titles boft,
Whilft I whome fortune of fuch tryumph bars
Vnlookt for ioy in that I honour n oft;
Great Princes fauorites their faire leaues fpread,
But as the Marygold at the funs eye,
And in them-felues their pride lies buried,
For at a frowne they in their glory die.
The painefull warrier famofed for worth,
After a thoufand victories once foild,
Is from the booke of honour rafed quite,
And all the reft forgot for which he toild:
    Then happy I that loue and am beloued
    Where I may not remoue, nor be remoued.

26

LOrd of my loue, to whome in vaffalage
Thy merrit hath my dutie ftrongly knit;
To thee I fend this written ambaffage
To witneffe duty, not to fhew my wit.
Duty fo great, which wit fo poore as mine
May make feeme bare, in wanting words to fhew it;
But that I hope fome good conceipt of thine
In thy foules thought (all naked) will beftow it:
Til whatfoeuer ftar that guides my mouing,
Points on me gratioufly with faire afpect,
And puts apparrell on my tottered louing,

C 2   **To**

Now begins a new series which will run through twenty-two sonnets without interruption.

The signal LOW links to his low esteem described in the adjacent text.

To finde where your true Image pictur'd lies,
Which in my bofomes fhop is hanging ftil,
That hath his windowes glazed with thine eyes:
Now fee what good-turnes eyes for eies haue done,
Mine eyes haue drawne thy fhape, and thine for me
Are windowes to my breft, where-through the Sun
Delights to peepe, to gaze therein on thee
 Yet eyes this cunning want to grace their art
 They draw but what they fee, know not the hart.

25

LEt thofe who are in fauor with their ftars,
 Of publike honour and proud titles boft,
Whilft I whome fortune of fuch tryumph bars
Vnlookt for ioy in that I honour moft ;
Great Princes fauorites their faire leaues fpread,
But as the Marygold at the funs eye,
And in them-felues their pride lies buried,
For at a frowne they in their glory die.
The painefull warrier famofed for worth,
After a thoufand victories once foild,
Is from the booke of honour rafed quite,
And all the reft forgot for which he toild :
 Then happy I that loue and am beloued
 Where I may not remoue, nor be remoued.

26

LOrd of my loue, to whome in vaffalage
 Thy merrit hath my dutie ftrongly knit ;
To thee I fend this written ambaffage
To witneffe duty, not to fhew my wit.
Duty fo great, which wit fo poore as mine
May make feeme bare, in wanting words to fhew it ;
But that I hope fome good conceipt of thine
In thy foules thought (all naked) will beftow it :
Til whatfoeuer ftar that guides my mouing,
Points on me gratioufly with faire afpect,
And puts apparrell on my tottered louing,
C 2

To

+

To show me worthy of their sweet respect,
　　Then may I dare to boast how I doe loue thee,
　　Til then,not show my head where thou maist proue me

27

WEary with toyle,I haste me to my bed,
　　The deare repose for lims with trauaill tired,
But then begins a iourny in my head
To worke my mind,when boddies work's expired.
For then my thoughts(from far where I abide)
Intend a zelous pilgrimage to thee,
And keepe my drooping eye-lids open wide,
Looking on darknes which the blind doe see.
Saue that my soules imaginary sight
Presents their shaddoe to my sightles view,
Which like a iewell(hunge in gastly night)
Makes blacke night beautious,and her old face new.
　　Loe thus by day my lims,by night my mind,
　　For thee,and for my selfe,noe quiet finde.

28

HOw can I then returne in happy plight
　　That am debard the benifit of rest?
When daies oppression is not eazd by night,
But day by night and night by day oprest.
And each(though enimes to ethers raigne)
Doe in consent shake hands to torture me,
The one by toyle,the other to complaine
How far I toyle,still farther off from thee.
I tell the Day to please him thou art bright,
And do'st him grace when clouds doe blot the heauen:
So flatter I the swart complexiond night,
When sparkling stars twire not thou guil'st th' eauen.
　　But day doth daily draw my sorrowes longer,(stronger
　　And night doth nightly make greefes length seeme

29

WHen in disgrace with Fortune and mens eyes,
　　I all alone beweepe my out-cast state,

And

Each letter is contained within one sonnet and each sonnet contains only one letter. However, the letters are indiscriminately tilted, inverted, and sometimes in mirror image.

To fhow me worthy of their fweet refpect,
  Then may I dare to boaft how I doe loue thee,
  Til then, not fhow my head where thou maift proue me.

27

WEary with toyle, I haft me to my bed,
  The deare repofe for lims with trauaill tired,
But then begins a iourny in my head
To worke my mind, when boddies work's expired.
For then my thoughts (from far where I abide)
Intend a zelous pilgrimage to thee,
And keepe my drooping eye-lids open wide,
Looking on darknes which the blind doe fee.
Saue that my foules imaginary fight
Prefents their fhaddoe to my fightles view,
Which like a iewell (hunge in gaftly night)
Makes blacke night beautious and her old face new.
  Loe thus by day my lims, by night my mind,
  For thee, and for my felfe, noe quiet finde.

28

HOw can I then returne in happy plight
  That am debard the benifit of reft ?
When daies oppreffion is not eazd by night,
But day by night and night by day opreft.
And each (though enimes to ethers raigne)
Doe in confent fhake hands to torture me,
The one by toyle, the other to complaine
How far I toyle, ftill farther off from thee.
I tell the Day to pleafe him thou art bright,
And do'ft him grace when clouds doe blot the heauen :
So flatter I the fwart complexiond night,
When fparkling ftars twire not thou guil'ft th' eauen.
  But day doth daily draw my forrowes longer, (ftronger
  And night doth nightly make greefes length feeme.

29

VVHen in difgrace with Fortune and mens eyes,
  I all alone beweepe my out-caft ftate,

                                              And

SONNETS.

And trouble deafe heauen with my bootlesse cries,
And looke vpon my selfe and curse my fate.
Wishing me like to one more rich in hope,
Featur'd like him,like him with friends possest,
Desiring this mans art,and that mans skope,
With what I most inioy contented least,
Yet in these thoughts my selfe almost despising,
Haplye I thinke on thee, and then my state,
(Like to the Larke at breake of daye arising)
From sullen earth sings himns at Heauens gate,
　　For thy sweet loue remembred such welth brings,
　　That then I skorne to change my state with Kings.

30

VVHen to the Sessions of sweet silent thought,
　　I sommon vp remembrance of things past,
I sigh the lacke of many a thing I sought,
And with old woes new waile my deare times waste:
Then can I drowne an eye(vn-vs'd to flow)
For precious friends hid in deaths dateles night,
And weepe a fresh loues long since canceld woe,
And mone th'expence of many a vannisht sight.
Then can I greeue at greeuances fore-gon,
And heauily from woe to woe tell ore
The sad account of fore-bemoned mone,
Which I new pay as if not payd before.
　　But if the while I thinke on thee (deare friend)
　　All losses are restord,and sorrowes end.

31

Thy bosome is indeared with all hearts,
　　Which I by lacking haue supposed dead,
And there raignes Loue and all Loues louing parts,
And all those friends which I thought buried.
How many a holy and obsequious teare
Hath deare religious loue stolne from mine eye,
As interest of the dead which now appeare,
But things remou'd that hidden in there lie,

　　　　　C 3　　　　　　　To

BUT in the margin links with itself starting with the same B.

This occurs fairly often, see Sonnet 133, as does the signal
AWT for aught.

And trouble deafe heauen with my bootleſſe cries,
And looke vpon my ſelfe and curſe my fate.
Wiſhing me like to one more rich in hope,
Featur'd like him, like him with friends poſſeſt,
Deſiring this mans art, and that mans skope,
With what I moſt inioy contented leaſt,
Yet in theſe thoughts my ſelfe almoſt deſpiſing,
Haplye I thinke on thee, and then my ſtate,
(Like to the Larke at breake of daye ariſing)
From ſullen earth ſings himns at Heauen's gate,
    For thy ſweet loue remembred ſuch welth brings,
    That then I skorne to change my ſtate with Kings.

30

VVHen to the Seſſions of ſweet ſilent thought,
    I ſommon vp remembrance of things paſt,
I ſigh the lacke of many a thing I ſought,
And with old woes new waile my deare times waſte :
Then can I drowne an eye (vn-vf'd to flow)
For precious friends hid in deaths dateles night,
And weepe a freſh loues long ſince canceld woe,
And mone th'expence of many a vanniſht ſight.
Then can I greeue at greeuances fore-gon,
And heauily from woe to woe tell ore
The ſad account of fore-bemoned mone,
Which I new pay as if not payd before.
    But if the while I thinke on thee (deare friend)
    All loſſes are reſtord, and ſorrowes end.

31

Thy boſome is indeared with all hearts ;
    Which I by lacking haue ſuppoſed dead,
And there raignes Loue and all Loues louing parts,
And all thoſe friends which I thought buried.
How many a holy and obſequious teare
Hath deare religious loue ſtolne from mine eye,
As intereſt of the dead, which now appeare,
But things remou'd that hidden in there lie,

C 3

To

54

Thou art the graue where buried loue doth liue,
Hung with the tropheis of my louers gon,
Who all their parts of me to thee did giue,
That due of many, now is thine alone.
   Their images I lou'd, I view in thee,
   And thou(all they)haft all the all of me.

32

IF thou furuiue my well contented daie,
  When that churle death my bones with duft fhall couer
And fhalt by fortune once more re-furuay:
Thefe poore rude lines of thy deceafed Louer:
Compare them with the bett'ring of the time,
And though they be out-ftript by euery pen,
Referue them for my loue, not for their rime,
Exceeded by the hight of happier men.
Oh then voutfafe me but this louing thought,
Had my friends Mufe growne with this growing age,
A dearer birth then this his loue had brought,
To march inranckes of better equipage:
   But fince he died and Poets better proue,
   Theirs for their ftile ile read,his for his loue.

P

33

FVll many a glorious morning haue I feene,
  Flatter the mountaine tops with foueraine eie,
Kiffing with golden face the meddowes greene;
Guilding pale ftreames with heauenly alcumy:
Anon permit the bafeft clouds to ride,
With ougly rack on his celeftiall face,
And from the for-lorne world his vifage hide
Stealing vnfeene to weft with this difgrace:
Euen fo my Sunne one early morne did fhine,
With all triumphant fplendor on my brow,
But out alack,he was but one houre mine,
The region cloude hath mask'd him from me now.
   Yet him for this,my loue no whit difdaineth,
   Suns of the world may ftaine,whē heauens fun ftainteh.

E

34

Note that six lines of Sonnet 31 carry over to this page but the
pace of one letter per Sonnet has been maintained.

Thou art the graue where buried loue doth liue,
Hung with the tropheis of my louers gon,
Who all their parts of me to thee did giue,
That due of many, now is thine alone.
   Their images I lou'd, I view in thee,
   And thou (all they) haſt all the all of me.

32

IF thou ſuruiue my well contented daie,
  When that churle death my bones with duſt ſhall couer
And ſhalt by fortune once more re-ſuruay :
Theſe poore rude lines of thy deceaſed Louer :
Compare them with the bett'ring of the time,
And though they be out-ſtript by euery pen,
Reſerue them for my loue, not for their rime,
Exceeded by the hight of happier men.
Oh then voutſafe me but this louing thought,
Had my friends Muſe growne with this growing age,
A dearer birth then this his loue had brought
To march in ranckes of better equipage :
   But ſince he died and Poets better proue,
   Theirs for their ſtile ile read, his for his loue.

33

FVll many a glorious morning haue I ſeene,
  Flatter the mountaine tops with ſoueraine eie,
Kiſſing with golden face the meddowes greene ;
Guilding pale ſtreames with heauenly alcumy :
Anon permit the baſeſt cloudes to ride,
With ougly rack on his celeſtiall face,
And from the for-lorne world his viſage hide
Stealing vnſeene to west with this diſgrace :
Euen ſo my Sunne one early morne did ſhine,
With all triumphant ſplendor on my brow,
But out alack, he was but one houre mine,
The region cloude hath mask'd him from me now.
   Yet him for this, my loue no whit diſdaineth,
   Suns of the world may ſtaine, whē heauens ſun ſtainteh.

                                     34

SONNETS.

34

WHy didst thou promise such a beautious day,
  And make me trauaile forth without my cloake,
To let bace cloudes ore-take me in my way,
Hiding thy brau'ry in their rotten smoke.
Tis not enough that through the cloude thou breake,
To dry the raine on my storme-beaten face,
For no man well of such a salue can speake,
That heales the wound, and cures not the disgrace:
Nor can thy shame giue phisicke to my griefe,
Though thou repent , yet I haue still the losse,
Th'offenders sorrow lends but weake reliefe
To him that beares the strong offenses losse.
  Ah but those teares are pearle which thy loue sheeds,
  And they are ritch,and ransome all ill deeds.

WAIT

A

35

NO more bee greeu'd at that which thou hast done,
  Roses haue thornes,and siluer fountaines mud,
Cloudes and eclipses staine both Moone and Sunne,
And loathsome canker liues in sweetest bud.
All men make faults,and euen I in this,
Authorizing thy trespas with compare,
My selfe corrupting saluing thy amisse,
Excusing their sins more then their sins are:
For to thy sensuall fault I bring in sence,
Thy aduerse party is thy Aduocate,
And gainst my selfe a lawfull plea commence,
Such ciuill war is in my loue and hate,
  That I an accessary needs must be,
  To that sweet theefe which sourely robs from me,

TASTE

R

36

LEt me confesse that we two must be twaine,
  Although our vndeuided loues are one:
So shall those blots that do with me remaine,
Without thy helpe , by me be borne alone.
In our two loues there is but one respect,

Though

In Sonnet 35 one namestick spans only three lines, from sunne in line three up to greeved in line one—uer. A poet may be allowed some license, especially in such a complex figure as the letter R.

34

VVHy didſt thou promiſe ſuch a beautious day,
   And make me trauaile forth without my cloake,
To let baſe cloudes ore-take me in my way,
Hiding thy brau'ry in their rotten ſmoke.
Tis not enough that through the cloude thou breake,
To dry the raine on my ſtorme-beaten face,
For no man well of ſuch a ſalue can ſpeake,
That heales the wound, and cures not the diſgrace :
Nor can thy ſhame giue phiſicke to my griefe,
Though thou repent, yet I haue ſtill the loſſe,
Th' offenders ſorrow lends but weake reliefe
To him that beares the ſtrong offenſes loſſe.
   Ah but thoſe teares are pearle which thy loue ſheeds,
   And they are ritch, and ranſome all ill deeds.

35

NO more bee greeu'd at that which thou haſt done,
   Roſes haue thornes, and ſiluer fountaines mud,
Cloudes and eclipſes ſtaine both Moone and Sunne,
And loathſome canker liues in ſweeteſt bud.
All men make faults, and euen I in this,
Authorizing thy treſpas with compare,
My ſelfe corrupting ſaluing thy amiſſe,
Excuſing their ſins more then their ſins are :
For to thy ſenſuall fault I bring in ſence,
Thy aduerſe party is thy Aduocate,
And gainſt my ſelfe a lawfull plea commence,
Such ciuill war is in my loue and hate,
   That I an acceſſary needs muſt be,
   To that ſweet theefe which ſourely robs from me,

36

LEt me confeſſe that we two muſt be twaine,
   Although our vndeuided loues are one :
So ſhall thoſe blots that do with me remaine,
Without thy helpe, by me be borne alone.
In our two loues there is but one reſpect,
                        Though

Though in our liues a seperable spight,
Which though it alter not loues sole effect,
Yet doth it steale sweet houres from loues delight,
I may not euer-more acknowledge thee,
Least my bewailed guilt should do thee shame,
Nor thou with publike kindnesse honour me,
Vnlesse thou take that honour from thy name:
　But doe not so, I loue thee in such sort,
　As thou being mine, mine is thy good report.

LIE

E

37

AS a decrepit father takes delight,
To see his actiue childe do deeds of youth,
So I, made lame by Fortunes dearest spight
Take all my comfort of thy worth and truth.
For whether beauty, birth, or wealth, or wit,
Or any of these all, or all, or more
Intitled in their parts, do crowned sit,
I make my loue ingrafted to this store:
So then I am not lame, poore, nor dispis'd,
Whilst that this shadow doth such substance giue,
That I in thy abundance am suffic'd,
And by a part of all thy glory liue:
　Looke what is best, that best I wish in thee,
　This wish I haue, then ten times happy me.

STAY

O

38

HOw can my Muse want subiect to inuent
While thou dost breath that poor'st into my verse,
Thine owne sweet argument, to excellent,
For euery vulgar paper to rehearse:
Oh giue thy selfe the thankes if ought in me,
Worthy perusal stand against thy sight,
For who's so dumbe that cannot write to thee,
When thou thy selfe dost giue inuention light?
Be thou the tenth Muse, ten times more in worth
Then those old nine which rimers inuocate,
And he that calls on thee, let him bring forth

OAF

X

Eternall

The pace of one letter per Sonnet is maintained. And now having finished W SHAKESPEARE he proceeds into OXFORD.

The signal OWF or Oaf is notable as a tip-off of some whimsy about to appear.

Though in our liues a feperable fpight,
Which though it alter not loues fole effect,
Yet doth it fteale fweet houres from loues delight,
I may not euer-more acknowledge thee,
Leaft my bewailed guilt fhould do thee fhame,
Nor thou with publike kindneffe honour me,
Vnleffe thou take that honour from thy name :
   But doe not fo, I loue thee in fuch fort,
   As thou being mine, mine is thy good report.

37

AS a decrepit father takes delight,
  To fee his actiue childe do deeds of youth,
So I, made lame by Fortunes deareft fpight
Take all my comfort of thy worth and truth.
For whether beauty, birth, or wealth, or wit,
Or any of thefe all, or all, or more
Intitled in their parts, do crowned fit,
I make my loue ingrafted to this ftore :
So then I am not lame, poore, nor difpif'd,
Whilft that this fhadow doth fuch fubftance giue,
That I in thy abundance am fuffic'd,
And by a part of all thy glory liue :
   Looke what is beft, that beft I wifh in thee,
   This wifh I haue, then ten times happy me.

38

HOw can my Mufe want fubiect to inuent
  While thou doft breath that poor'ft into my verfe,
Thine owne fweet argument, to excellent,
For euery vulgar paper to rehearfe :
Oh giue thy felfe the thankes if ought in me,
Worthy perufal ftand againft thy fight,
For who's fo dumbe that cannot write to thee,
When thou thy felfe doft giue inuention light ?
Be thou the tenth Mufe, ten times more in worth
Then thofe old nine which rimers inuocate,
And he that calls on thee, let him bring forth
                       Eternall

SONNETS.

Eternal numbers to out-liue long date.
    If my flight Muse doe pleafe thefe curious daies,
    The paine be mine, but thine fhal be the praife.

39

OH how thy worth with manners may I finge,
    When thou art all the better part of me?
What can mine owne praife to mine owne felfe bring;
And what is't but mine owne when I praife thee,
Euen for this, let vs deuided liue,
And our deare loue loofe name of fingle one,
That by this feperation I may giue:
That due to thee which thou deferu'ft alone:
Oh abfence what a torment wouldft thou proue,
Were it not thy foure leifure gaue fweet leaue,
To entertaine the time with thoughts of loue,
VVhich time and thoughts fo fweetly doft deceiue.
    And that thou teacheft how to make one twaine,
    By praifing him here who doth hence remaine.

40

TAke all my loues, my loue, yea take them all,
    What haft thou then more then thou hadft before?
No loue, my loue, that thou maift true loue call,
All mine was thine, before thou hadft this more:
Then if for my loue, thou my loue receiueft,
I cannot blame thee, for my loue thou vfeft,
But yet be blam'd, if thou this felfe deceaueft
By wilfull tafte of what thy felfe refufeft.
I doe forgiue thy robb'rie gentle theefe
Although thou fteale thee all my pouerty:
And yet loue knowes it is a greater griefe
To beare loues wrong, then hates knowne iniury.
    Lafciuious grace, in whom all il wel fhowes,
    Kill me with fpights yet we muft not be foes.

41

THofe pretty wrongs that liberty commits,
    When I am fome-time abfent from thy heart,

D   Thy

F

O

BITE

The ideas of eating, biting and tasting appear also in the Signals and Links in Sonnets 35 and 66.

Eternal numbers to out-liue long date.
 If my flight Mufe doe pleafe thefe curious daies,
 The paine be mine, but thine fhall be the praife.

39

OH how thy worth with manners may I finge,
 When thou art all the better part of me ?
What can mine owne praife to mine owne felfe bring ;
And what is't but mine owne when I praife thee,
Euen for this, let vs deuided liue,
And our deare loue loofe name of fingle one,
That by this feperation I may giue :
That due to thee which thou deferu'ft alone :
Oh abfence what a torment wouldft thou proue,
Were it not thy foure leifure gaue fweet leaue,
To entertaine the time with thoughts of loue,
VVhich time and thoughts fo fweetly doft deceiue.
 And that thou teacheft how to make one twaine,
 By praifing him here who doth hence remaine.

40

TAke all my loues, my loue, yea take them all,
 What haft thou then more then thou hadft before ?
No loue, my loue, that thou maift true loue call,
All mine was thine, before thou hadft this more :
Then if for my loue, thou my loue receiueft,
I cannot blame thee, for my loue thou vfeft,
But yet be blam'd, if thou this felfe deceaueft
By wilfull tafte of what thy felfe refufeft.
I doe forgiue thy robb'rie gentle theefe
Although thou fteale thee all my pouerty :
And yet loue knowes it is a greater griefe
To beare loues wrong, then hates knowne iniury.
 Lafciuious grace, in whom all il wel fhowes,
 Kill me with fpights yet we muft not be foes.

41

THofe pretty wrongs that liberty commits,
 When I am fome-time abfent from thy heart,
    D   Thy

62

Thy beautie,and thy yeares full well befits,
For still temptation followes where thou art.
Gentle thou art,and therefore to be wonne,
Beautious thou art,therefore to be assailed.
And when a woman woes,what womans sonne,
Will sourely leaue her till he haue preuailed.
Aye me but yet thou mightst my seate forbeare,
And chide thy beauty,and thy straying youth,
Who lead thee in their ryot euen there
Where thou art forst to breake a two-fold truth:
  Hers by thy beauty tempting her to thee,
  Thine by thy beautie beeing false to me.

AWAY

R

42

THat thou hast her it is not all my griefe,
  And yet it may be said I lou'd her deerely,
That she hath thee is of my wayling cheefe,
A losse in loue that touches me more neerely.
Louing offendors thus I will excuse yee,
Thou doost loue her,because thou know'st I loue her,
And for my sake euen so doth she abuse me,
Suffring my friend for my sake to approoue her,
If I loose thee,my losse is my loues gaine,
And loosing her,my friend hath found that losse,
Both finde each other,and I loose both twaine,
And both for my sake lay on me this crosse,
  But here's the ioy,my friend and I are one,
  Sweete flattery,then she loues but me alone.

JAB

D

43

WHen most I winke then doe mine eyes best see,
  For all the day they view things vnrespected,
But when I sleepe,in dreames they looke on thee,
And darkely bright,are bright in darke directed.
Then thou whose shaddow shaddowes doth make bright,
How would thy shadowes forme,forme happy show,
To the cleere day with thy much cleerer light,
When to vn-seeing eyes thy shade shines so?

V

How

After finishing OXORD the letters begin to spell VERE with
an inverted V.

Thy beautie, and thy yeares full well befits,
For ftill temptacion followes where thou art.
Gentle thou art, and therefore to be wonne,
Beautious thou art, therefore to be affailed.
And when a woman woes, what womans fonne,
Will fourely leaue her till he haue preuailed.
Aye me, but yet thou mighft my feate forbeare,
And chide thy beauty, and thy ftraying youth,
Who lead thee in their ryot euen there
Where thou are forft to breake a two-fold truth :
 Hers by thy beauty tempting her to thee,
 Thine by thy beautie beeing falfe to me.

42

THat thou haft her it is not all my griefe,
 And yet it may be faid I lou'd her deerely,
That fhe hath thee is of my wayling cheefe,
A loffe in loue that touches me more neerely.
Louing offendors thus I will excufe yee,
Thou dooft loue her, becaufe thou knowft I loue her,
And for my fake euen fo doth fhe abufe me,
Suffring my friend for my fake to approoue her,
If I loofe thee, my loffe is my loues gaine,
And loofing her, my friend hath found that loffe,
Both finde each other, and I loofe both twaine,
And both for my fake lay on me this croffe,
 But here's the ioy, my friend and I are one,
 Sweete flattery, then fhe loues but me alone.

43

WHen moft I winke then doe mine eyes beft fee,
 For all the day they view things vnrefpected,
But when I fleepe, in dreames they looke on thee,
And darkely bright, are bright in darke directed.
Then thou whofe fhaddow fhaddowes doth make bright,
How would thy fhaddowes forme, forme happy fhow,
To the cleere day with thy much cleerer light,
When to vn-feeing eyes thy fhade fhines fo ?

           How

SONNETS.

How would (I fay)mine eyes be bleſſed made,
By looking on thee in the liuing day?
When in dead night their faire imperfect ſhade,
Through heauy ſleepe on ſightleſſe eyes doth ſtay?
  A'l dayes are nights to ſee till I ſee thee,
  And nights bright daies when dreams do ſhew thee me,

44

IF the dull ſubſtance of my fleſh were thought,
Iniurious diſtance ſhould not ſtop my way,
For then diſpight of ſpace I would be brought,
From limits farre remote,where thou dooſt ſtay,
No matter then although my foote did ſtand
Vpon the fartheſt earth remoou'd from thee,
For nimble thought can iumpe both ſea and land,
As ſoone as thinke the place where he would be.
But ah,thought kills me that I am not thought
To leape large lengths of miles when thou art gone,
But that ſo much of earth and water wrought,
I muſt attend,times leaſure with my mone.
  Receiuing naughts by elements ſo ſloe,
  But heauie teares,badges of eithers woe.

45

THe other two,ſlight ayre,and purging fire,
Are both with thee,where euer I abide,
The firſt my thought,the other my deſire,
Theſe preſent abſent with ſwift motion ſlide.
For when theſe quicker Elements are gone
In tender Embaſſie of loue to thee,
My life being made of foure,with two alone,
Sinkes downe to death,oppreſt with melancholie.
Vntill liues compoſition be recured,
By theſe ſwift meſſengers return'd from thee,
Who euen but now come back againe aſſured,
Of their faire health,recounting it to me.
  This told,I ioy,but then no longer glad,
  I ſend them back againe and ſtraight grow ſad.

D 2   Mine

Again a bad break in Sonnet 43 with six lines to spare but the pace goes on.

How would (I fay) mine eyes be bleffed made,
By looking on thee in the liuing day?
When in dead night their faire imperfeſt fhade,
Through heauy fleepe on fightleffe eyes doth ftay?
　　All dayes are nights to fee till I fee thee,
　　And nights bright daies when dreams do fhew thee me.

44

IF the dull fubftance of my flefh were thought,
Iniurious diftance fhould not ftop my way,
For then difpight of fpace I would be brought,
From limits farre remote, where thou dooft ftay,
No matter then although my foote did ftand
Vpon the fartheft earth remoou'd from thee,
For nimble thought can iumpe both fea and land,
As foone as thinke the place where he would be.
But ah, thought kills me that I am not thought
To leape large lengths of miles when thou art gone,
But that fo much of earth and water wrought,
I muft attend, times leafure with my mone.
　　Receiuing naughts by elements fo floe,
　　But heauie teares, badges of eithers woe.

45

THe other two, flight ayre, and purging fire,
Are both with thee, where euer I abide,
The firft my thought, the other my defire,
Thefe prefent abfent with fwift motion flide.
For when thefe quicker Elements are gone
In tender Embaffie of loue to thee,
My life being made of foure, with two alone,
Sinkes downe to death, oppreft with melancholie.
Vntill liues compofition be recured,
By thofe fwift meffengers return'd from thee,
Who euen but now come back againe affured,
Of their faire health, recounting it to me.
　　This told, I ioy, but then no longer glad,
　　I fend them back againe and ftraight grow fad.

Mine

46

MIne eye and heart are at a mortall warre,
How to deuide the conquest of thy sight,
Mine eye, my heart their pictures sight would barre,
My heart, mine eye the freedome of that right,
My heart doth plead that thou in him doost lye,
(A closet neuer pearst with christall eyes)
But the defendant doth that plea deny,
And sayes in him their faire appearance lyes.
To side this title is impannelled
A quest of thoughts, all tennants to the heart,
And by their verdict is determined
The cleere eyes moytie, and the deare hearts part.
　As thus, mine eyes due is their outward part,
　And my hearts right, their inward loue of heart.

ABATE

E

47

BEtwixt mine eye and heart a league is tooke,
And each doth good turnes now vnto the other,
When that mine eye is famisht for a looke,
Or heart in loue with sighes himselfe doth smother;
With my loues picture then my eye doth feast,
And to the painted banquet bids my heart:
An other time mine eye is my hearts guest,
And in his thoughts of loue doth share a part.
So either by thy picture or my loue,
Thy seife away, are present still with me,
For thou nor farther then my thoughts canst moue,
And I am still with them, and they with thee.
　Or if they sleepe, thy picture in my sight
　Awakes my heart, to hearts and eyes delight.

48

HOw carefull was I when I tooke my way,
Each trifle vnder truest barres to thrust,
That to my vse it might vn-vsed stay
From hands of falsehood, in sure wards of trust?
But thou, to whom my iewels trifles are,

Most

The figure in Sonnet 47 appears to be a little stick-man taking his bow, as well he might.

46

MIne eye and heart are at a mortall warre,
How to deuide the conqueſt of thy ſight,
Mine eye, my heart their pictures ſight would barre,
My heart, mine eye the freeedome of that right,
My heart doth plead that thou in him dooſt lye,
(A cloſet neuer pearſt with chriſtall eyes)
But the defendant doth that plea deny,
And ſayes in him their faire appearance lyes.
To ſide this title is impannelled
A queſt of thoughts, all tennants to the heart,
And by their verdict is determined
The cleere eyes moyitie, and the deare hearts part.
  As thus, mine eyes due is their outward part,
  And my hearts right, their inward loue of heart.

47

BEtwixt mine eye and heart a league is tooke,
And each doth good turnes now vnto the other,
When that mine eye is famiſht for a looke,
Or heart in loue with ſighes himſelfe doth ſmother;
With my loues picture then my eye doth feaſt,
And to the painted banquet bids my heart:
An other time mine eye is my hearts gueſt,
And in his thoughts of loue doth ſhare a part.
So either by thy picture or my loue,
Thy ſeife away, are preſent ſtill with me,
For thou nor farther then my thoughts canſt moue,
And I am ſtill with them, and they with thee.
  Or if they ſleepe, thy picture in my ſight
  Awakes my heart, to hearts and eyes delight.

48

HOw carefull was I when I tooke my way,
Each trifle vnder trueſt barres to thruſt,
That to my vſe it might vn-vſed ſtay
From hands of falſehood, in ſure wards of truſt?
But thou, to whom my iewels trifles are,

Moſt

SONNETS.

Moſt worthy comfort, now my greateſt griefe,
Thou beſt of deereſt, and mine onely care,
Art left the prey of euery vulgar theefe.
Thee haue I not lockt vp in any cheſt,
Saue where thou art not though I feele thou art,
Within the gentle cloſure of my breſt,
From whence at pleaſure thou maiſt come and part,
    And euen thence thou wilt be ſtolne I feare,
    For truth prooues theeuiſh for a prize ſo deare.

49

AGainſt that time (if euer that time come)
    When I ſhall ſee thee frowne on my defects,
When as thy loue hath caſt his vtmoſt ſumme,
Cauld to that audite by aduiſ'd reſpects,
Againſt that time when thou ſhalt ſtrangely paſſe,
And ſcarcely greete me with that ſunne thine eye,
When loue conuerted from the thing it was
Shall reaſons finde of ſetled grauitie.
Againſt that time do I inſconce me here
Within the knowledge of mine owne deſart,
And this my hand, againſt my ſelfe vpreare,
To guard the lawfull reaſons on thy part,
    To leaue poore me, thou haſt the ſtrength of lawes,
    Since why to loue, I can alledge no cauſe.

50

HOw heauie doe I iourney on the way,
    When what I ſeeke (my wearie trauels end)
Doth teach that eaſe and that repoſe to ſay
Thus farre the miles are meaſurde from thy friend.
The beaſt that beares me, tired with my woe,
Plods duly on, to beare that waight in me,
As if by ſome inſtinct the wretch did know
His rider lou'd not ſpeed being made from thee:
The bloody ſpurre cannot prouoke him on,
That ſome-times anger thruſts into his hide,
Which heauily he anſwers with a grone,

D 3   More

Here is DE V along with warnings in the signals STA and
WAT. Something more is about to make its appearance. The
signal PAHT is onomatopoeia for the sound of a plodding
beast.

'Moſt worthy comfort, now my greateſt griefe,
Thou beſt of deereſt, and mine onely care,
Art left the prey of euery vulgar theefe.
Thee haue I not lockt vp in any cheſt,
Saue where thou art not though I feele thou art,
Within the gentle cloſure of my breſt,
From whence at pleaſure thou maiſt come and part,
   And euen thence thou wilt be ſtolne I feare,
   For truth prooues theeuiſh for a prize ſo deare.

49

A Gainſt that time (if euer that time come)
   When I ſhall ſee thee frowne on my defects,
When as thy loue hath caſt his vtmoſt ſumme,
Cauld to that audite by aduiſ'd reſpects,
Againſt that time when thou ſhalt ſtrangely paſſe,
And ſcarcely greete me with that ſunne thine eye,
When loue conuerted from the thing it was
Shall reaſons finde of ſetled grauitie.
Againſt that time do I inſconce me here
Within the knowledge of mine owne deſart,
And this my hand, againſt my ſelfe vpreare,
To guard the lawfull reaſons on thy part,
   To leaue poore me, thou haſt the ſtrength of lawes,
   Since why to loue, I can alledge no cauſe.

50

How heauie doe I iourney on the way,
   When what I ſeeke (my wearie trauels end)
Doth teach that eaſe and that repoſe to ſay
Thus farre the miles are meaſurde from thy friend.
The beaſt that beares me, tired with my woe,
Plods duly on, to beare that waight in me,
As if by ſome inſtinct the wretch did know
His rider lou'd not ſpeed being made from thee :
The bloody ſpurre cannot prouoke him on,
That ſome-times anger thruſts into his hide,
Which heauily he anſwers with a grone,
      D 3   More

SHAKE-SPEARES.

More sharpe to me then spurring to his side,
  For that same grone doth put this in my mind,
  My greefe lies onward and my ioy behind.

51

THus can my loue excuse the slow offence,
  Of my dull bearer, when from thee I speed,
From where thou art, why shoulld I hast me thence,
Till I returne of posting is noe need.
O what excuse will my poore beast then find,
When swift extremity can seeme but slow,
Then should I spurre though mounted on the wind,
In winged speed no motion sha'l I know,
Then can no horse with my desire keepe pace,
Therefore desire (of perfects loue being made)
Shall naigh noe dull flesh in his fiery race,
But loue, for loue, thus shall excuse my iade,
  Since from thee going, he went wilfull slow,
  Towards thee ile run, and giue him leaue to goe.

52

SO am I as the rich whose blessed key,
  Can bring him to his sweet vp-locked treasure,
The which he will not eu'ry hower suruay,
For blunting the fine point of seldome pleasure.
Therefore are feasts so sollemne and so rare,
Since sildom comming in the long yeare set,
Like stones of worth they thinly placed are,
Or captaine Iewells in the carconet.
So is the time that keepes you as my chest,
Or as the ward-robe which the robe doth hide,
To make some speciall instant speciall blest,
By new vnfoulding his imprison'd pride.
  Blessed are you whose worthinesse giues skope,
  Being had to tryumph, being lackt to hope.

53

VVHat is your substance, whereof are you made,
  That millions of strange shaddowes on you tend?

Since

This is the beginning of a sequence spelling WILLIAM
SHAKESPEARE with all the letters blocked out by double
lines. The marginal signals tell us there will be TWO lines
used and that it will go SLO; no longer will the one sonnet-
one letter pace be kept.

More sharpe to me then spurring to his side,
  For that same grone doth put this in my mind,
  My greefe lies onward and my ioy behind.

51

THus can my loue excuse the slow offence,
  Of my dull bearer, when from thee I speed,
From where thou art, why shoulld I hast me thence,
Till I returne of posting is noe need.
O what excuse will my poore beast then find,
When swift extremity can seeme but slow,
Then should I spurre though mounted on the wind,
In winged speed no motion shall I know,
Then can no horse with my desire keepe pace,
Therefore desire (of perfects loue being made)
Shall naigh noe dull flesh in his fiery race,
But loue, for loue, thus shall excuse my iade,
  Since from thee going he went wilfull slow,
  Towards thee ile run, and giue him leaue to goe.

52

SO am I as the rich whose blessed key,
  Can bring him to his sweet vp-locked treasure,
The which he will not eu'ry hower suruay,
For blunting the fine point of seldome pleaure.
Therefore are feasts so sollemne and so rare,
Since sildom comming in the long yeare set,
Like stones of worth they thinly placed are,
Or captaine Iewells in the carconet.
So is the time that keepes you as my chest,
Or as the ward-robe which the robe doth hide,
To make some speciall instant speciall blest,
By new vnfoulding his imprison'd pride.
  Blessed are you whose worthinesse giues skope,
  Being had to tryumph, being lackt to hope.

53

VVHat is your substance, whereof are you made,
  That millions of strange shaddowes on you tend?
                                              Since

SONNETS.

Since euery one,hath euery one,one fhade,
And you but one,can euery fhaddow lend:
Defcribe *Adonis* and the counterfet,
Is poorely immitated after you,
On *Hellens* cheeke all art of beautie fet,
And you in *Grecian* tires are painted new:
Speake of the fpring,and foyzon of the yeare,
The one doth fhaddow of your beautie fhow,
The other as your bountie doth appeare,
And you in euery bleffed fhape we know.
   In all externall grace you haue fome part,
   But you like none,none you for conftant heart.

I

54

OH how much more doth beautie beautious feeme,
  By that fweet ornament which truth doth giue,
The Rofe lookes faire, but fairer we it deeme
For that fweet odor,which doth in it liue:
The Canker bloomes haue full as deepe a die,
As the perfumed tincture of the Rofes,
Hang on fuch thornes,and play as wantonly,
When fommers breath their masked buds difclofes:
But for their virtue only is their fhow,
They liue vnwoo'd, and vnrefpected fade,
Die to themfelues . Sweet Rofes doe not fo,
Of their fweet deathes, are fweeteft odors made:
   And fo of you,beautious and louely youth,
   When that fhall vade,by verfe diftils your truth.

L

55

NOt marble, nor the guilded monument,
  Of Princes fhall out-liue this powrefull rime,
But you fhall fhine more bright in thefe contents
Then vnfwept ftone, befmeer'd with fluttifh time.
When waftefull warre fhall *Statues* ouer-turne,
And broiles roote out the worke of mafonry,
Nor *Mars* his fword, nor warres quick fire fhall burne .
The liuing record of your memory.

                             Gainft

NAUGHT

The absolute symmetry of the letter W on the preceeding
page represents a standard too high to be maintained. Allow-
ance has to be made as the letters progress for variations from
true parallelism and equal spacing of the namesticks.

Since euery one, hath euery one, one fhade,
And you but one, can euery fhaddow lend :
Defcribe *Adonis* and the counterfet,
Is poorely immitated after you,
On *Hellens* cheeke all art of beautie fet,
And you in *Grecian* tires are painted new :
Speake of the fpring, and foyzon of the yeare,
The one doth fhaddow of your beautie fhow,
The other as your bountie doth appeare,
And you in euery blefled fhape we know.
   In all externall grace you haue fome part,
   But you like none, none you for conftant heart.

54

OH how much more doth beautie beautious feeme,
  By that fweet ornament which truth doth giue,
The Rofe lookes faire, but fairer we it deeme
For that fweet odor, which doth in it liue :
The Canker-bloomes haue full as deepe a die,
As the perfumed tincture of the Rofes,
Hang on fuch thornes, and play as wantonly,
When fommers breath their masked buds difclofes :
But for their virtue only is their fhow,
They liue vnwoo'd, and vnrefpected fade,
Die to themfelues . Sweet Rofes doe not fo,
Of their fweet deathes, are fweeteft odors made :
   And fo of you, beautious and louely youth,
   When that fhall vade, by verfe diftils your truth.

55

NOt marble, nor the guilded monument,
  Of Princes fhall out-liue this powrefull rime,
But you fhall fhine more bright in thefe contents
Then vnfwept ftone, befmeer'd with fluttifh time.
When waftefull warre fhall *Statues* ouer-turne,
And broiles roote out the worke of mafonry,
Nor *Mars* his fword, nor warres quick fire fhall burne :
The liuing record of your memory.

                       Gainft

SHAKE-SPEARES.

Gainst death, and all obliuious emnity
Shall you pace forth, your praise shall stil finde roome,
Euen in the eyes of all posterity
That weare this world out to the ending doome.
    So til the iudgement that your selfe arise,
    You liue in this, and dwell in louers eies.

56

SWeet loue renew thy force, be it not said
Thy edge should blunter be then apetite,
Which but too daie by feeding is alaied,
To morrow sharpned in his former might.
So loue be thou, although too daie thou fill
Thy hungrie eies, euen till they winck with fulnesse,
Too morrow see againe, and doe not kill
The spirit of Loue, with a perpetual dulnesse:
Let this sad Intrim like the Ocean be
Which parts the shore, where two contracted new,
Come daily to the banckes, that when they see:
Returne of loue, more blest may be the view.
    As cal it Winter, which being ful of care,
    Makes Somers welcome, thrice more wish'd, more rare:

L

CULT

57

BEing your slaue what should I doe but tend,
Vpon the houres, and times of your desire?
I haue no precious time at al to spend;
Nor seruices to doe til you require.
Nor dare I chide the world without end houre,
Whilst I (my soueraine) watch the clock for you,
Nor thinke the bitternesse of absence sowre,
VVhen you haue bid your seruant once adieue.
Nor dare I question with my iealious thought,
VVhere you may be, or your affaires suppose,
But like a sad slaue stay and thinke of nought
Saue where you are, how happy you make those.
    So true a foole is loue, that in your Will,
    (Though you doe any thing) he thinkes no ill.

I

58

The linking idea is sometimes a direct opposite to the signal as here in SET and ARISE.

The use of namesticks seven and eight lines long in Sonnet 57 by aligning names in tandem emphasizes the intent to form a block letter I. The poet has indulged his license for one of the forms by using E (for Edward) VER.

Gainft death, and all obliuious emnity
Shall you pace forth, your praife fhall ftil finde roome,
Euen in the eyes of all pofterity
That weare this world out to the ending doome.
   So til the iudgement that your felfe arife,
   You liue in this, and dwell in louers eies.

56

Sweet loue renew thy force, be it not faid
Thy edge fhould blunter be then apetite,
Which but too daie by feeding is alaied,
To morrow fharpned in his former might.
So loue be thou, although too daie thou fill
Thy hungrie eies, euen till they winck with fulneffe,
Too morrow fee againe, and doe not kill
The fpirit of Loue, with a perpetual dulneffe :
Let this fad *Intrim* like the Ocean be
Which parts the fhore, where two contracted new,
Come daily to the banckes, that when they fee :
Returne of loue, more bleft may be the view.
   As cal it Winter, which being ful of care,
   Makes Sómers welcome, thrice more wifh'd, more rare :

57

BEing your flaue what fhould I doe but tend,
Vpon the houres, and times of your defire ?
I haue no precious time at al to fpend ;
Nor feruices to doe til you require.
Nor dare I chide the world without end houre,
Whilft I (my foueraine) watch the clock for you,
Nor thinke the bitterneffe of abfence fowre,
VVhen you haue bid your feruant once adieue.
Nor dare I queftion with my ieallous thought,
VVhere you may be, or your affaires fuppofe,
But like a fad flaue ftay and thinke of nought
Saue where you are, how happy you make thofe.
   So true a foole is loue, that in your Will,
   (Though you doe any thing) he thinkes no ill.

58

THat God forbid, that made me firſt your ſlaue,
I ſhould in thought controule your times of pleaſure,
Or at your hand th' account of houres to craue,
Being your vaſſail bound to ſtaie your leiſure,
Oh let me ſuffer(being at your beck)
Th' impriſon'd abſence of your libertie,
And patience tame,to ſufferance bide each check.
Without accuſing you of iniury.
Be where you liſt,your charter is ſo ſtrong,
That you your ſelfe may priuiledge your time
To what you will,to you it doth belong,
Your ſelfe to pardon of ſelfe-doing crime.
   I am to waite,though waiting ſo be hell,
   Not blame your pleaſure be it ill or well.

A

WAIT

59

IF there bee nothing new,but that which is,
Hath beene before , how are our braines beguild,
Which laboring for inuention beare amiſſe
The ſecond burthen of a former child ?
Oh that record could with a back-ward looke,
Euen of fiue hundreth courſes of the Sunne,
Show me your image in ſome antique booke,
Since minde at firſt in carrecter was done.
That I might ſee what the old world could ſay,
To this compoſed wonder of your frame,
Whether we are mended,or where better they,
Or whether reuolution be the ſame.
   Oh ſure I am the wits of former daies,
   To ſubiects worſe haue giuen admiring praiſe.

60

LIke as the waues make towards the pibled ſhore,
So do our minuites haſten to their end,
Each changing place with that which goes before,
In ſequent toile all forwards do contend.
Natuity once in the maine of light,

E   Crawle

The formation of a block letter A presents a difficult problem and the solution here lacks brilliance. Note, however, the resort to a subterfuge—the badly mis-spelled word carrecter (Sonnet 59 line 8), ostensibly overlooked by the proofreader —but which is needed to provide an e for the lowermost name-stick. The author used the normal spelling—character—in other places.

Again the signals give the reader warning not to pass up this page and to look for a letter formed with TWO lines.

58

THat God forbid, that made me firſt your ſlaue,
　I ſhould in thought controule your times of pleaſure
Or at your hand th' account of houres to craue,
Being your vaſſail bound to ſtaie your leiſure.
Oh let me ſuffer (being at your beck)
Th' impriſon'd abſence of your libertie,
And patience tame, to ſufferance bide each check,
Without accuſing you of iniury.
Be where you liſt, your charter is ſo ſtrong,
That you your ſelfe may priuiledge your time
To what you will, to you it doth belong,
Your ſelfe to pardon of ſelfe-doing crime.
　　I am to waite, though waiting ſo be hell,
　　Not blame your pleaſure be it ill or well.

59

IF their bee nothing new, but that which is,
　Hath beene before, how are our braines beguild,
Which laboring for inuention beare amiſſe
The ſecond burthen of a former child?
Oh that record could with a back-ward looke,
Euen of fiue hundreth courſes of the Sunne,
Show me your image in ſome antique booke,
Since minde at firſt in carreċter was done.
That I might ſee what the old world could ſay,
To this compoſed wonder of your frame,
Whether we are mended, or where better they,
Or whether reuolution be the ſame.
　　Oh ſure I am the wits of former daies,
　　To ſubieċts worſe haue giuen admiring praiſe.

60

LIke as the waues make towards the pibled ſhore,
　So do our minuites haſten to their end,
Each changing place with that which goes before,
In ſequent toile all forwards do contend.
Natuity once in the maine of light.
　　　　　　　　　E　　　　　　　　Crawls

SHAKESPEARES

Crawles to maturity, where with being crown'd,
Crooked eclipses gainst his glory fight,
And time that gaue, doth now his gift confound.
Time doth transfixe the florish set on youth,
And delues the paralels in beauties brow,
Feedes on the rarities of natures truth,
And nothing stands but for his sieth to mow.
 And yet to times in hope, my verse shall stand
 Praising thy worth, disright his cruell hand.

61

IS it thy wil, thy Image should keepe open
 My heauy eie ids to the weary night?
Dost thou desire my slumbers should be broken,
While shadowes like to thee do mocke my sight?
Is it thy spirit that thou send'st from thee
So farre from home into my deeds to prye,
To find out shames and idle houres in me,
The skope and tenure of thy Ielousie?
O no, thy loue though much, is not so great,
It is my loue that keepes mine eie awake,
Mine owne true loue that doth my rest defeat,
To plaie the watch-man euer for thy sake.
 For thee watch I, whilst thou dost wake elsewhere,
 From me farre of, with others all to neere.

62

SInne of selfe-loue possesseth al mine eie,
 And all my soule, and al my euery part;
And for this sinne there is no remedie,
It is so grounded inward in my heart.
Me thinkes no face so gratious is as mine,
No shape so true, no truth of such account,
And for my selfe mine owne worth do define,
As I all other in all worths surmount.
But when my glasse shewes me my selfe indeed
Beated and chopt with tand antiquitie,
Mine owne selfe loue quite contrary I read

Selfe

TOY

NAY

M

The signal FAT refers to the construction of the large letters
and will be found again several times.

Crawles to maturity, wherewith being crown'd,
Crooked eclipfes gainft his glory fight,
And time that gaue, doth now his gift confound.
Time doth tranffixe the florifh fet on youth,
And delues the paralels in beauties brow,
Feedes on the rarities of natures truth,
And nothing ſtands but for his ſieth to mow.
  And yet to times in hope, my verfe fhall ftand
  Praifing thy worth, difpight his cruell hand.

61

IS it thy wil, thy Image fhould keepe open
  My heauy eielids to the weary night?
Doft thou defire my flumbers fhould be broken,
While fhadowes like to thee do mocke my fight?
Is it thy fpirit that thou fend'ft from thee
So farre from home into my deeds to prye,
To find out fhames and idle houres in me,
The skope and tenure of thy Ieloufie?
O no, thy loue though much, is not fo great,
It is my loue that keepes mine eie awake,
Mine owne true loue that doth my reft defeat,
To plaie the watch-man euer for my fake.
  For thee watch I, whilft thou doft wake elfewhere,
  From me farre of, with others all to neere.

62

SInne of felfe-loue poffeffeth al mine eie,
  And all my foule, and al my euery part;
And for this finne there is no remedie,
It is fo grounded inward in my heart.
Me thinkes no face fo gratious is as mine,
No fhape fo true, no truth of fuch account,
And for my felfe mine owne worth to define,
As I all other in all worths furmount.
But when my glaffe fhewes me my felfe indeed
Beated and chopt with tand antiquitie,
Mine owne felfe loue quite contrary I read

                                            Selfe

80

SONNETS.

Selfe,fo felfe louing were iniquity,
T'is thee(my felfe)that for my felfe I praife,
Painting my age with beauty of thy daies.

63

AGainft my loue fhall be as I am now
With times iniurious hand chrufht and ore-worne,
When houres haue dreind his blood and fild his brow
With lines and wrincles,when his youthfull morne
Hath trauaild on to Ages fteepie night,
And all thofe beauties whereof now he's King
Are vanifhing,or vanifht out of fight,
Stealing away the treafure of his Spring.
For fuch a time do I now fortifie
Againft confounding Ages cruell knife,
That he fhall neuer cut from memory
My fweet loues beauty,though my louers life.
His beautie fhall in thefe blacke lines be feene,
And they fhall liue, and he in them ftill greene.

64

VVHen I haue feene by times fell hand defaced
The rich proud coft of outworne buried age,
When fometime loftie towers I fee downe rafed,
And braffe eternall flaue to mortall rage.
When I haue feene the hungry Ocean gaine
Aduantage on the Kingdome of the fhoare,
And the firme foile win of the watry maine,
Increafing ftore with loffe,and loffe with ftore.
When I haue feene fuch interchange of ftate,
Or ftate it felfe confounded, to decay,
Ruine hath taught me thus to ruminate
That Time will come and take my loue away.
This thought is as a death which cannot choofe
But weepe to haue,that which it feares to loofe.

65

SInce braffe,nor ftone,nor earth,nor boundleffe fea,
But fad mortallity ore-fwaies their power,

E 2   How

Here is the signal FAT again signalling the continued formation of block letters.

Selfe, fo felfe louing were iniquity,
  T'is thee (my felfe) that for my felfe I praife,
  Painting my age with beauty of thy daies.

63

A Gainſt my loue ſhall be as I am now
  With times iniurious hand chruſht and ore-worne,
When houres haue dreind his blood and fild his brow
With lines and wrincles, when his youthfull morne
Hath trauaild on to Ages ſteepie night,
And all thoſe beauties whereof now he's King
Are vaniſhing, or vaniſht out of ſight,
Stealing away the treaſure of his Spring.
For ſuch a time do I now fortifie
Againſt confounding Ages cruell knife,
That he ſhall neuer cut from memory
My ſweet loues beauty, though my louers life.
  His beautie ſhall in these blacke lines be ſeene,
  And they ſhall liue, and he in them ſtill greene.

64

VVHen I haue ſeene by times fell hand defaced
  The rich proud coſt of outworne buried age,
When ſometime loftie towers I ſee downe raſed,
And braſſe eternall ſlaue to mortall rage.
When I haue ſeene the hungry Ocean gaine
Aduantage on the Kingdome of the ſhoare,
And the firme ſoile win of the watry maine,
Increaſing ſtore with loſſe, and loſſe with ſtore.
When I haue ſeene ſuch interchange of ſtate,
Or ſtate it ſelfe confounded, to decay,
Ruine hath taught me thus to ruminate
That Time will come and take my loue away.
  This thought is as a death which cannot chooſe
  But weepe to haue, that which it feares to looſe.

65

SInce braſſe, nor ſtone, nor earth, nor boundleſſe ſea,
  But ſad mortallity ore-ſwaies their power,

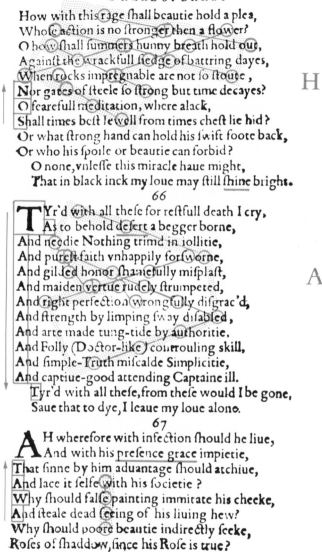

How with this rage shall beautie hold a plea,
Whose action is no stronger then a flower?
O how shall summers hunny breath hold out,
Against the wrackfull siedge of battring dayes,
When rocks impregnable are not so stoute ,
Nor gates of steele so strong but time decayes?
O fearefull meditation, where alack,
Shall times best Iewell from times chest lie hid ?
Or what strong hand can hold his swift foote back,
Or who his spoile or beautie can forbid ?
    O none, vnlesse this miracle haue might,
    That in black inck my loue may still shine bright.

66

TYr'd with all these for restfull death I cry,
    As to behold desert a begger borne,
And needie Nothing trimd in iollitie,
And purest faith vnhappily forsworne,
And gilded honor shamefully misplast,
And maiden vertue rudely strumpeted,
And right perfection wrongfully disgrac'd,
And strength by limping sway disabled ,
And arte made tung-tide by authoritie,
And Folly (Doctor-like) controuling skill,
And simple-Truth miscalde Simplicitie,
And captiue-good attending Captaine ill.
    Tyr'd with all these, from these would I be gone,
    Saue that to dye, I leaue my loue alone.

67

AH wherefore with infection should he liue,
    And with his presence grace impietie,
That sinne by him aduantage should atchiue,
And lace it selfe with his societie ?
Why should false painting immitate his cheeke,
And steale dead seeing of his liuing hew?
Why should poore beautie indirectly seeke,
Roses of shaddow, since his Rose is true?

Why

Here is a whimsical change of pace in the margin. T-A's-T is pronounced "taste" and links to "desert."

The page break in Sonnet 67 makes a block letter impossible but he gives the instruction AWAIT and links it to the idea of waiting in the Queen's presence chamber.

How with this rage fhall beautie hold a plea,
Whofe aċtion is no ftronger then a flower?
O how fhall fummers hunny breath hold out,
Againft the wrackfull fiedge of battring dayes,
When rocks impregnable are not fo ftoute,
Nor gates of fteele fo ftrong but time decayes?
O fearefull meditation, where alack,
Shall times beft Iewell from times cheft lie hid?
Or what ftrong hand can hold his fwift foote back,
Or who his fpoile or beautie can forbid?
   O none, vnleffe this miracle haue might,
   That in black inck my loue may ftill fhine bright.

66

TYr'd with all thefe for reftfull death I cry,
  As to behold defert a begger borne,
And needie Nothing trimd in iollitie,
And pureft faith vnhappily forfworne,
And gilded honor fhamefully mifplaft,
And maiden vertue rudely ftrumpeted,
And right perfeċtion wrongfully difgrac'd,
And ftrength by limping fway difabled,
And arte made tung-tide by authoritie,
And Folly (Doċtor-like) controuling skill,
And fimple-Truth mifcalde Simplicitie,
And captiue-good attending Captaine ill.
   Tyr'd with all thefe, from thefe would I be gone;
   Saue that to dye, I leaue my loue alone.

67

AH wherefore with infeċtion fhould he liue,
  And with his prefence grace impietie,
That finne by him aduantage fhould atchiue,
And lace it felfe with his focietie?
Why fhould falfe painting immitate his cheeke,
And fteale dead feeing his ofliuing hew?
Why fhould poore beautie indireċtly feeke,
Rofes of fhaddow, fince his Rofe is true?

                           Why

SONNETS.

Why should he liue,now nature banckrout is,
Beggerd of blood to blush through liuely vaines,
For she hath no exchecker now but his,
And proud of many,liues vpon his gaines?
O him she stores,to show what welth she had,
In daies long since,before these last so bad.

68

THus is his cheeke the map of daies out-worne,
    When beauty liu'd and dy'ed as flowers do now,
Before these bastard signes of faire were borne,
Or durst inhabit on a liuing brow:
Before the goulden tresses of the dead,
The right of sepulchers,were shorne away,
To liue a scond life on second head,
Ere beauties dead fleece made another gay:
In him those holy antique howers are seene,
Without all ornament,it selfe and true,
Making no summer of an others greene,
Robbing no ould to dresse his beauty new,
    And him as for a map doth Nature store,
    To shew faulse Art what beauty was of yore.

K

69

THose parts of thee that the worlds eye doth view,
    Want nothing that the thought of hearts can mend:
All toungs(the voice of soules)giue thee that end,
Vttring bare truth,euen so as foes Commend.
Their outward thus with outward praise is crownd,
But those same toungs that giue thee so thine owne,
In other accents doe this praise confound
By seeing farther then the eye hath showne.
They looke into the beauty of thy mind,
And that in guesse they measure by thy deeds,
Then churls their thoughts(although their eies were kind)
To thy faire flower ad the rancke smell of weeds,
    But why thy odor matcheth not thy show,
    The solye is this,that thou doest common grow.

E

AUGHT

E 3   That

Here in the other fragment of Sonnet 67 he, in effect, calls
himself an OAF for allowing this split-up. Again he is faithful
to his system of signal—link and namestick. For confirmation
of the OAF exclamation, note the next page.

Why fhould he liue, now nature banckrout is,
Beggerd of blood to blufh through liuely vaines,
For fhe hath no exchecker now but his,
And proud of many, liues vpon his gaines ?
 O him fhe ftores, to fhow what welth fhe had,
 In daies long fince, before thefe laft fo bad.

68

THus is his cheeke the map of daies out-worne,
 When beauty liu'd and dy'ed as flowers do now,
Before thefe baftard fignes of faire were borne,
Or durft inhabit on a liuing brow :
Before the goulden treffes of the dead,
The right of fepulchers, were fhorne away,
To liue a fecond life on fecond head,
Ere beauties dead fleece made another gay :
In him thofe holy antique howers are feene,
Without all ornament, it felfe and true,
Making no fummer of an others greene,
Robbing no ould to dreffe his beauty new,
 And him as for a map doth Nature ftore,
 To fhew faulfe Art what beauty was of yore.

69

THofe parts of thee that the worlds eye doth view,
 Want nothing that the thought of hearts can mend :
All toungs (the voice of foules) giue thee that end,
Vttring bare truth, euen fo as foes Commend.
Their outward thus with outward praife is crownd,
But thofe fame toungs that giue thee fo thine owne,
In other accents doe this praife confound
By feeing farther then the eye hath fhowne.
They looke into the beauty of thy mind,
And that in gueffe they meafure by thy deeds,
Then churls their thoughts (although their eies were kind)
To thy faire flower ad the rancke fmell of weeds,
 But why thy odor matcheth not thy fhow,
 The foyle is this, that thou doeft common grow.

70

THat thou are blam'd shall not be thy defect,
For slanders marke was euer yet the faire,
The ornament of beauty is suspect,
A Crow that flies in heauens sweetest ayre,
So thou be good, slander doth but approue,
Their worth the greater beeing woo'd of time,
For Canker vice the sweetest buds doth loue,
And thou present'st a pure vnstayined prime.
Thou hast past by the ambush of young daies,
Either not assayld, or victor beeing charg'd,
Yet this thy praise cannot be soe thy praise,
To tye vp enuy, euermore inlarged,
    If some suspect of ill maskt not thy show,
    Then thou alone kingdomes of hearts shouldst owe.

S

71

NOe Longer mourne for me when I am dead,
Then you shall heare the surly sullen bell
Giue warning to the world that I am fled
From this vile world with vildest wormes to dwell:
Nay if you read this line, remember not,
The hand that writ it, for I loue you so,
That I in your sweet thoughts would be forgot,
If thinking on me then should make you woe.
O if (I say) you looke vpon this verse,
When I (perhaps) compounded am with clay,
Do not so much as my poore name reherse;
But let your loue euen with my life decay.
    Least the wise world should looke into your mone,
    And mocke you with me after I am gon.

P

VOID

72

OLeast the world should taske you to recite,
What merit liu'd in me that you should loue
After my death (deare loue) for get me quite,
For you in me can nothing worthy proue.
Valesse you would deuise some vertuous lye,

To

Another awkward page break and again the expletive OAF.
There are many, many examples in the plays where an acrostic
ploy which might be doubted is confirmed by immediate
repetition.

70

THat thou are blam'd ſhall not be thy defeꝏ,
  For ſlanders marke was euer yet the faire,
The ornament of beauty is ſuſpeꝏ,
A Crow that flies in heauens ſweeteſt ayre.
So thou be good, ſlander doth but approue,
Their worth the greater beeing woo'd of time,
For Canker vice the ſweeteſt buds doth loue,
And thou preſent'ſt a pure vnſtayined prime.
Thou haſt paſt by the ambuſh of young daies,
Either not aſſayld, or viꝏor beeing charg'd,
Yet this thy praiſe cannot be ſoe thy praiſe,
To tye vp enuy, euermore inlarged,
   If ſome ſuſpeꝏ of ill maskt not thy ſhow,
   Then thou alone kingdomes of hearts ſhouldſt owe.

71

NOe Longer mourne for me when I am dead,
  Then thou ſhall heare the ſurly ſullen bell
Giue warning to the world that I am fled
From this vile world with vildeſt wormes to dwell :
Nay if you read this line, remember not,
The hand that writ it, for I loue you ſo,
That I in your ſweet thoughts would be forgot,
If thinking on me then ſhould make you woe.
O if (I ſay) you looke vpon this verſe,
When I (perhaps) compounded am with clay,
Do not ſo much as my poore name reherſe ;
But let your loue euen with my life decay.
   Leſt the wiſe world ſhould looke into your mone,
   And mocke you with me after I am gon.

72

O Leaſt the world ſhould taske you to recite,
  What merit liu'd in me that you ſhould loue
After my death (deare loue) for get me quite,
For you in me can nothing worthy proue.
Vnleſſe you would deuiſe ſome vertuous lye,

                           To

SONNETS.

To doe more for me then mine owne defert,
And hang more praife vpon deceafed I,
Then nigard truth would willingly impart:
O leaft your true loue may feeme falce in this,
That you for loue fpeake well of me vntrue,
My name be buried where my body is,
And liue no more to fhame nor me,nor you.
For I am fhamd by that which I bring forth,
And fo fhould you,to loue things nothing worth.

73

THat time of yeeare thou maift in me behold,
 When yellow leaues,or none,or few doe hange
Vpon thofe boughes which fhake againft the could,
Bare rn'wd quiers,where late the fweet birds fang,
In me thou feeft the twi-light of fuch day,
As after Sun-fet fadeth in the Weft,
Which by and by blacke night doth take away,
Deaths fecond felfe that feals vp all in reft,
In me thou feeft the glowing of fuch fire,
That on the afhes of his youth doth lye,
As the death bed,whereon it muft expire,
Confum'd with that which it was nurrifht by.
 This thou perceu'ft,which makes thy loue more ftrong,
 To loue that well,which thou muft leaue erelong.

74

BVt be contented when that fell areft,
 With out all bayle fhall carry me away,
My life hath in this line fome intereft,
Which for memoriall ftill with thee fhall ftay.
When thou reueweft this,thou doeft reuew,
The very part was confecrate to thee,
The earth can haue but earth,which is his due,
My fpirit is thine the better part of me,
So then thou haft but loft the dregs of life,
The pray of wormes,my body being dead,
The coward conqueft of a wretches knife,

To

At last a well formed block A. The block E and R are also of
higher standards than the last preceeding letters.

To doe more for me then mine owne defert,
And hang more praife vpon deceafed I,
Then nigard truth would willingly impart :
O leaft your true loue may feeme falce in this,
That yuo for loue fpeake well of me vntrue,
My name be buried where my body is,
And liue no more to fhame nor me, nor you.
   For I am fhamd by that which I bring forth,
   And fo fhould you, to loue things nothing worth.

73

THat time of yeeare thou maift in me behold,
  When yellow leaues, or none, or few doe hange
Vpon thofe boughes which fhake againft the could,
Bare rn'wd quiers, where late the fweet birds fang.
In me thou feeft the twi-light of fuch day,
As after Sun-fet fadeth in the Weft,
Which by and by blacke night doth take away,
Deaths fecond felfe that feals vp all in reft.
In me thou feeft the glowing of fuch fire,
That on the afhes of his youth doth lye,
As the death bed, whereon it muft expire,
Confum'd with that which it was nurrifht by.
   This thou perceu'ft, which makes thy loue more ftrong,
   To loue that well, which thou muft leaue ere long.

74

BVt be contented when that fell areft,
  With out all bayle fhall carry me away,
My life hath in this line fome intereft,
Which for memoriall ftill with thee fhall ftay.
When thou reueweft this, thou doeft reuew,
The very part was confecrate to thee,
The earth can haue but earth, which is his due,
My fpirit is thine the better part of me,
So then thou haft but loft the dregs of life,
The pray of wormes, my body being dead,
The coward conqueft of a wretches knife,

                                        To

To bafe of thee to be remembred,
>   The worth of that,is that which it containes,
>   And that is this, and this with thee remaines.

75

SO are you to my thoughts as food to life,
Or as fweet feafon'd fhewers are to the ground;
And for the peace of you I hold fuch ftrife,
As twixt a mifer and his wealth is found.
Now proud as an inioyer,and anon
Doubting the filching age will fteale his treafure,
Now counting beft to be with you alone,
Then betterd that the world may fee my pleafure,
Some-time all ful with feafting on your fight,
And by and by cleane ftarued for a looke,
Poffeffing or purfuing no delight
Saue what is had,or muft from you be tooke.
>   Thus do I pine and furfet day by day,
>   Or gluttoning on all,or all away,

76

VVHy is my verfe fo barren of new pride?
>   So far from variation or quicke change?
Why with the time do I not glance afide
To new found methods,and to compounds ftrange?
Why write I ftill all one,euer the fame,
And keepe inuention in a noted weed,
That euery word doth almoft fel my name,
Shewing their birth,and where they did proceed?
O know fweet loue I alwaies write of you,
And you and loue are ftill my argument:
So all my beft is dreffing old words new,
Spending againe what is already fpent:
>   For as the Sun is daily new and old,
>   So is my loue ftill telling what is told,

77

THy glaffe will fhew thee how thy beauties were,
Thy dyall how thy pretious mynuits wafte,

The

The final block E is made by an easier method, that is, by adopting the form of the script capital "E." Likewise the signal SOA and link "so."

Here as he proceeds immediately into a W SHAKESPEARE in simple letters he gives the warning WAT again.

To bafe of thee to be remembred,
  The worth of that, is that which it containes,
  And that is this, and this with thee remaines.

75

SO are you to my thoughts as food to life,
  Or as fweet feafon'd fhewers are to the ground ;
And for the peace of you I hold fuch ftrife,
As twixt a mifer and his wealth is found.
Now proud as an inioyer, and anon
Doubting the filching age will fteale his treafure,
Now counting beft to be with you alone,
Then betterd that the world may fee my pleafure,
Some-time all ful with feafting on your fight,
And by and by cleane ftarued for a looke,
Poffefling or purfuing no delight
Saue what is had, or muft from you be tooke.
  Thus do I pine and furfet day by day,
  Or gluttoning on all, or all away,

76

VVHy is my verfe fo barren of new pride ?
  So far from variation or quicke change ?
Why with the time do I not glance afide
To new found methods, and to compounds ftrange ?
Why write I ftill all one, euer the fame,
And keepe inuention in a noted weed,
That euery word doth almoft fel my name,
Shewing their birth, and where they did proceed ?
O know fweet loue I alwaies write of you,
And you and loue are ftill my argument :
So all my beft is dreffing old words new,
Spending againe what is already fpent :
  For as the Sun is daily new and old,
  So is my loue ftill telling what is told,

77

THy glaffe will fhew thee how thy beauties were,
  Thy dyall how thy pretious mynuits wafte,
                     The

SONNETS.

The vacant leaues thy mindes imprint will beare,
And of this booke, this learning maift thou tafte,
The wrinckles which thy glaffe will truly fhow,
Of mouthed graues will giue thee memorie,
Thou by thy dyals fhady ftealth maift know,
Times theeuifh progreffe to eternitie.
Looke what thy memorie cannot containe,
Commit to thefe wafte blacks, and thou fhalt finde
Thofe children nurft, deliuerd from thy braine,
To take a new acquaintance of thy minde.
   Thefe offices, fo oft as thou wilt looke,
   Shall profit thee, and much inrich thy booke.

S

78

SO oft haue I inuok'd thee for my Mufe,
  And found fuch faire affiftance in my verfe,
As euery Alien pen hath got my vfe,
And vnder thee their poefie difperfe.
Thine eyes, that taught the dumbe on high to fing,
And heauie ignorance aloft to flie,
Haue added fethers to the learneds wing,
And giuen grace a double Maieftie.
Yet be moft proud of that which I compile,
Whofe influence is thine, and borne of thee,
In others workes thou dooft but mend the ftile,
And Arts with thy fweete graces graced be.
   But thou art all my art, and dooft aduance
   As high as learning, my rude ignorance.

H

79

WHilft I alone did call vpon thy ayde,
  My verfe alone had all thy gentle grace,
But now my gracious numbers are decayde,
And my fick Mufe doth giue an other place.
I grant (fweet loue)thy louely argument
Deferues the trauaile of a worthier pen,
Yet what of thee thy Poet doth inuent,
He robs thee of, and payes it thee againe,

F

A

He

An interesting question in Sonnet 79, where the same word is
spelled AID in the margin and "Ayde" in the text, is whether
the short spelling at that time was known or was an Oxfordian
phoneticism which ultimately coincided with modern spelling.

The vacant leaues thy mindes imprint will beare,
And of this booke, this learning maiſt thou taſte.
The wrinckles which thy glaſſe will truly ſhow,
Of mouthed graues will giue thee memorie,
Thou by thy dyals ſhady ſtealth maiſt know,
Times theeuiſh progreſſe to eternitie.
Looke what thy memorie cannot containe,
Commit to theſe waſte blacks, and thou ſhalt finde
Thoſe children nurſt, deliuerd from thy braine,
To take a new acquaintance of thy minde.
  Theſe offices, ſo oft as thou wilt looke,
  Shall profit thee, and much inrich thy booke.

78

SO oft haue I inuok'd thee for my Muſe,
  And found ſuch faire aſſiſtance in my verſe,
As euery *Alien* pen hath got my vſe,
And vnder thee their poeſie diſperſe.
Thine eyes, that taught the dumbe on high to ſing,
And heauie ignorance aloft to flee,
Haue added fethers to the learneds wing,
And giuen grace a double Maieſtie.
Yet be moſt proud of that which I compile,
Whoſe influence is thine, and borne of thee,
In others workes thou dooſt but mend the ſtile,
And Arts with thy ſweete graces graced be.
  But thou art all my art, and dooſt aduance
  As high as learning, my rude ignorance.

79

WHilſt I alone did call vpon thy ayde,
  My verſe alone had all thy gentle grace,
But now my gracious numbers are decayde,
And my ſick Muſe doth giue an other place.
I grant (ſweet loue) thy louely argument
Deſerues the trauaile of a worthier pen,
Yet what of thee thy Poet doth inuent,
He robs thee of, and payes it thee againe,

F   He

SHAKE-SPEARES

FAINT

He lends thee vertue, and he ſtole that word,
From thy behauiour, beautie doth he giue
And found it in thy cheeke: he can affoord
No praiſe to thee, but what in thee doth liue.
   Then thanke him not for that which he doth ſay,
   Since what he owes thee, thou thy ſelfe dooſt pay,

K

80

O How I faint when I of you do write,
   Knowing a better ſpirit doth vſe your name,
And in the praiſe thereof ſpends all his might,
To make me toung-tide ſpeaking of your fame.
But ſince your worth (wide as the Ocean is)
The humble as the proudeſt ſaile doth beare,
My ſawſie barke (inferior farre to his)
On your broad maine doth wilfully appeare.
Your ſhalloweſt helpe will hold me vp a floate,
Whilſt he vpon your ſoundleſſe deepe doth ride,
Or (being wrackt) I am a worthleſſe bote,
He of tall building, and of goodly pride.
   Then If he thriue and I be caſt away,
   The worſt was this, my loue was my decay.

E

THOU

&1

FATE

OR I ſhall liue your Epitaph to make,
   Or you ſuruiue when I in earth am rotten,
From hence your memory death cannot take,
Although in me each part will be forgotten.
Your name from hence immortall life ſhall haue,
Though I (once gone) to all the world muſt dye,
The earth can yeeld me but a common graue,
When you intombed in mens eyes ſhall lye,
Your monument ſhall be my gentle verſe,
Which eyes not yet created ſhall ore-read,
And toungs to be, your beeing ſhall rehearſe,
When all the breathers of this world are dead,
   You ſtill ſhall liue (ſuch vertue hath my Pen)
   Where breath moſt breaths, euen in the mouths of men.

S

I grant

FANT is the only example where the signal is in one Sonnet and the link is in the next one (faint).

FAYT in Sonnet 81 was apparently spelled this way to distinguish from the several instances of FAT and yet to avoid too frequent use of four letter signals in straight-forward spelling.

He lends thee vertue, and he ſtole that word,
From thy behauiour, beautie doth he giue
And found it in thy cheeke : he can affoord
No praiſe to thee, but what in thee doth liue.
　Then thanke him not for that which he doth ſay,
　Since what he owes thee, thou thy ſelfe dooſt pay,

80

O How I faint when I of you do write,
　Knowing a better ſpirit doth vſe your name,
And in the praiſe thereof ſpends all his might,
To make me toung-tide ſpeaking of your fame.
But ſince your worth (wide as the Ocean is)
The humble as the proudeſt ſaile doth beare,
My ſawſie barke (inferior farre to his)
On your broad maine doth wilfully appeare.
Your ſhalloweſt helpe will hold me vp a floate,
Whilſt he vpon your ſoundleſſe deepe doth ride,
Or (being wrackt) I am a worthleſſe bote,
He of tall building, and of goodly pride.
　Then If he thriue and I be caſt away,
　The worſt was this, my loue was my decay.

81

OR I ſhall liue your Epitaph to make,
　Or you ſuruiue when I in earth am rotten,
From hence your memory death cannot take,
Although in me each part will be forgotten.
Your name from hence immortall life ſhall haue,
Though I (once gone) to all the world muſt dye,
The earth can yeeld me but a common graue,
When you intombed in mens eyes ſhall lye,
Your monument ſhall be my gentle verſe,
Which eyes not yet created ſhall ore-read,
And toungs to be, your beeing ſhall rehearſe,
When all the breathers of this world are dead,
　You ſtill ſhall liue (ſuch vertue hath my Pen)
　Where breath moſt breaths, euen in the mouths of men.

I grant

SONNETS.

82

I Grant thou wert not married to my Mufe,
  And therefore maieſt without attaint ore-looke
The dedicated words which writers vſe
Of their faire ſubieċt,bleſſing euery booke.
Thou art as faire in knowledge as in hew,
Finding thy worth a limmit paſt my praiſe,
And therefore art inforc'd to ſeeke anew,
Some freſher ſtampe of the time bettering dayes.
And do ſo loue,yet when they haue deuiſde,
What ſtrained touches Rhethorick can lend,
Thou truly faire,wert truly ſimpathizde,
In true plaine words,by thy true telling friend.
  And their groſſe painting might be better vſ'd,
  Where cheekes need blood,in thee it is abuſ'd.

P

83

I Neuer ſaw that you did painting need,
  And therefore to your faire no painting ſet,
I found (or thought I found) you did exceed,
The barren tender of a Poets debt :
And therefore haue I ſlept in your report,
That you your ſelfe being extant well might ſhow,
How farre a moderne quill doth come to ſhort,
Speaking of worth,what worth in you doth grow,
This ſilence for my ſinne you did impute,
Which ſhall be moſt my glory being dombe,
For I impaire not beautie being mute,
When others would giue life,and bring a tombe.
  There liues more life in one of your faire eyes,
  Then both your Poets can in praiſe deuiſe.

E

84

W Ho is it that ſayes moſt,which can ſay more,
  Then this rich praiſe,that you alone,are you,
In whoſe confine immured is the ſtore,
Which ſhould example where your equall grew,
Leane penurie within that Pen doth dwell,

F 2   That

Whimsy appears again in the SH—"silence" of Sonnet 83 and
the self-applause in using WIT for the next signal.

82

I Grant thou wert not married to my Mufe,
  And therefore maieft without attaint ore-looke
The dedicated words which writers vfe
Of their faire fubiect, bleffing euery booke.
Thou art as faire in knowledge as in hew,
Finding thy worth a limmit paft my praife,
And therefore art inforc'd to feeke anew,
Some frefher ftampe of the time bettering dayes.
And do fo loue, yet when they haue deuifde,
What ftrained touches Rhethorick can lend,
Thou truly faire, wert truly fimpathizde,
In true plaine words, by thy true telling friend.
    And their groffe painting might be better vf'd,
    Where cheekes need blood, in thee it is abuf'd.

83

I Neuer faw that you did painting need,
  And therefore to your faire no painting fet,
I found (or thought I found) you did exceed,
The barren tender of a Poets debt :
And therefore haue I flept in your report,
That you your felfe being extant well might fhow,
How farre a moderne quill doth come to fhort,
Speaking of worth, what worth in you doth grow,
This filence for my finne you did impute,
Which fhall be moft my glory being dombe,
For I impaire not beautie being mute,
When others would giue life, and bring a tombe.
    There liues more life in one of your faire eyes,
    Then both your Poets can in praife deuife.

84

W Ho is it that fayes moft, which can fay more,
   Then this rich praife, that you alone, are you,
In whofe confine immured is the ftore,
Which fhould example where your equall grew,
Leane penurie within that Pen doth dwell,

F 2   That

That to his fubiect lends not fome fmall glory,
But he that writes of you,if he can tell,
That you are you,fo dignifies his ftory.
Let him but coppy what in you is writ,
Not making worfe what nature made fo cleere,
And fuch a counter-part fhall fame his wit,
Making his ftile admired euery where.
  You to your beautious bleffings adde a curfe,
  Being fond on praife,which makes your praifes worfe.

NAME

A

85

MY toung-tide Mufe in manners holds her ftill,
While comments of your praife richly compil'd,
Referue their Character with goulden quill,
And precious phrafe by all the Mufes fil'd.
I thinke good thoughts,whilft other write good wordes,
And like vnlettered clarke ftill crie Amen,
To euery Himne that able fpirit affords,
In polifht forme of well refined pen.
Hearing you praifd,I fay 'tis fo, 'tis true,
And to the moft of praife adde fome-thing more,
But that is in my thought,whofe loue to you
(Though words come hind-moft)holds his ranke before,
  Then others,for the breath of words refpect,
  Me for my dombe thoughts,fpeaking in effect.

RAJAH

R

86

WAs it the proud full faile of his great verfe,
Bound for the prize of (all to precious) you,
That did my ripe thoughts in my braine inhearce,
Making their tombe the wombe wherein they grew?
Was it his fpirit,by fpirits taught to write,
Aboue a mortall pitch,that ftruck me dead ?
No,neither he,nor his compiers by night
Giuing him ayde,my verfe aftonifhed.
He nor that affable familiar ghoft
Which nightly gulls him with intelligence,
As victors of my filence cannot boaft,

VAIN

E

I was

Oxford would have known of the "ranke" of RAJA(H). He
was a heavy investor in exploratory voyages and apparently
followed the affairs of the new East India Company.

That to his fubiect lends not fome fmall glory,
But he that writes of you, if he can tell,
That you are you, fo dignifies his ftory.
Let him but coppy what in you is writ,
Not making worfe what nature made fo cleere,
And fuch a counter-part fhall fame his wit,
Making his ftile admired euery where.
 You to your beautious bleffings adde a curfe,
 Being fond on praife, which makes your praifes worfe.

85

MY toung-tide Mufe in manners holds her ftill,
While comments of your praife richly compil'd,
Referue their Character with goulden quill,
And precious phrafe by all the Mufes fil'd.
I thinke good thoughts, whilft other write good wordes,
And like vnlettered clarke ftill crie Amen,
To euery Himne that able fpirit affords,
In polifht forme of well refined pen.
Hearing you praifd, I fay 'tis fo, 'tis true,
And to the moft of praife adde fome-thing more,
But that is in my thought, whofe loue to you
(Though words come hind-moft) holds his ranke before,
 Then others, for the breath of words refpect,
 Me for my dombe thoughts, fpeaking in effect.

86

VVAs it the proud full faile of his great verfe,
Bound for the prize of (all to precious) you,
That did my ripe thoughts in my braine inhearce,
Making their tombe the wombe wherein they grew ?
Was it his fpirit, by fpirits taught to write,
Aboue a mortall pitch, that ftruck me dead ?
No, neither he, nor his compiers by night
Giuing him ayde, my verfe aftonifhed.
He nor that affable familiar ghoft
Which nightly gulls him with intelligence,
As victors of my filence cannot boaft,

 I was

100

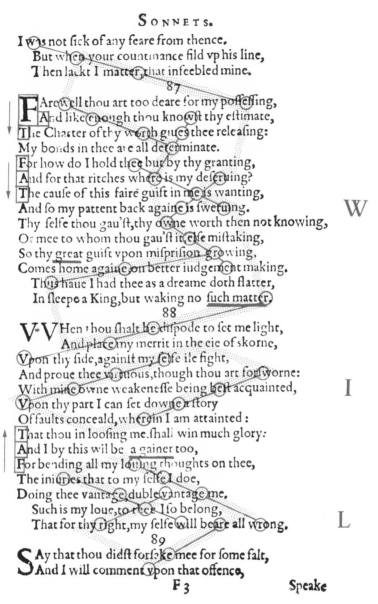

I was not sick of any feare from thence,
  But when your countinance fild vp his line,
  Then lackt I matter, that infeebled mine.

87

FArewell thou art too deare for my possessing,
  And like enough thou knowst thy estimate,
The Charter of thy worth giues thee releasing:
My bonds in thee are all determinate.
For how do I hold thee but by thy granting,
And for that ritches where is my deseruing?
The cause of this faire guift in me is wanting,
And so my pattent back againe is sweruing.
Thy selfe thou gau'st,thy owne worth then not knowing,
Or mee to whom thou gau'st it else mistaking,
So thy great guift vpon misprision growing,
Comes home againe on better iudgement making.
  Thus haue I had thee as a dreame doth flatter,
  In sleepe a King,but waking no such matter.

88

WHen thou shalt be dispode to set me light,
  And place my merrit in the eie of skorne,
Vpon thy side,against my selfe ile fight,
And proue thee virtuous,though thou art forsworne:
With mine owne weakenesse being best acquainted,
Vpon thy part I can set downe a story
Of faults conceald,wherein I am attainted :
That thou in loosing me shall win much glory:
And I by this wil be a gainer too,
For bending all my louing thoughts on thee,
The iniuries that to my selfe I doe,
Doing thee vantage,duble vantage me.
  Such is my loue,to thee I so belong,
  That for thy right,my selfe will beare all wrong.

89

SAy that thou didst forsake mee for some falt,
  And I will comment vpon that offence,

F3   Speake

W

I

L

Sonnet 87 starts a new sequence of "fat" letters and to make
certain it won't be missed the signal FAT appears in the margin three times.

47838

I was not fick of any feare from thence.
But when your countinance fild vp his line,
Then lackt I matter, that infeebled mine.

87

FArewell thou art too deare for my poffeffing,
And like enough thou knowft thy eftimate,
The Charter of thy worth giues thee releafing :
My bonds in thee are all determinate.
For how do I hold thee but by thy granting,
And for that ritches where is my deferuing ?
The caufe of this faire guift in me is wanting,
And fo my pattent back againe is fweruing.
Thy felfe thou gau'ft, thy owne worth then not knowing,
Or mee to whom thou gau'ft it, elfe miftaking,
So thy great guift vpon mifprifion growing,
Comes home againe, on better iudgement making.
    Thus haue I had thee as a dreame doth flatter,
    In fleepe a King, but waking no fuch matter.

88

VVHen thou fhalt be difpode to fet me light,
And place my merrit in the eie of skorne,
Vpon thy fide, againft my felfe ile fight,
And proue thee virtuous, though thou art forfworne :
With mine owne weakeneffe being beft acquainted,
Vpon thy part I can fet downe a ftory
Of faults conceald, wherein I am attainted :
That thou in loofing me fhall win much glory :
And I by this wil be a gainer too,
For bending all my louing thoughts on thee,
The iniuries that to my felfe I doe,
Doing thee vantage, duble vantage me.
    Such is my loue, to thee I fo belong,
    That for thy right, my felfe will beare all wrong,

89

SAy that thou didft forfake mee for fome falt,
And I will comment vpon that offence,

F 3   The

Lincoln Christian College

SHAKE-SPEARES

Speake of my lamenesse, and I straight will halt:
Against thy reasons making no defence.
Thou canst not(loue)disgrace me halfe so ill,
To set a forme vpon desired change,
As ile my selfe disgrace, knowing thy wil,
I will acquaintance strangle and looke strange:
Be absent from thy walkes and in my tongue,
Thy sweet beloued name no more shall dwell,
Least I(too much prophane)should do it wronge:
And haplie of our old acquaintance tell.
    For thee,against my selfe ile vow debate,
    For I must nere loue him whom thou dost hate.

                    90

THen hate me when thou wilt, if euer,now,
Now while the world is bent my deeds to crosse,
Ioyne with the spight of fortune,make me bow,
And doe not drop in for an after losse:
Ah doe not,when my heart hath scapte this sorrow
Come in the rereward of a conquerd woe,
Giue not a windy night a rainie morrow,
To linger out a purposd ouer-throw.
If thou wilt leaue me, do not leaue me last,
When other pettie griefes haue done their spight,
But in the onset come,so shall I taste
At first the very worst of fortunes might.
    And other straines of woe, which now seeme woe,
    Compar'd with losse of thee,will not seeme so.

                    91

SOme glory in their birth,some in their skill,
Some in their wealth, some in their bodies force,
Some in their garments though new-fangled ill:
Some in their Hawkes and Hounds,some in their Horse.
And euery humor hath his adiunct pleasure,
Wherein it findes a ioy aboue the rest,
But these perticulers are not my measure,
All these I better in one generall best.

                                        Thy

FAULT

L

I

A

M

Apparently the signal WIT calls attention to the feat of squeezing four block letters onto one page.

Speake of my lamenefle, and I ftraight will halt :
Againft thy reafons making no defence.
Thou canft not (loue) difgrace me halfe fo ill,
To fet a forme vpon defired change,
As ile my felfe difgrace, knowing thy wil,
I will acquaintance ftrangle and looke ftrange :
Be abfent from thy walkes and in my tongue,
Thy fweet beloued name no more fhall dwell,
Leaft I (too much prophane) fhould do it wronge :
And haplie of our old acquaintance tell.
    For thee, againft my feelfe ile vow debate,
    For I muft nere loue him whom thou doft hate.

90

THen hate me when thou wilt, if euer, now,
    Now while the world is bent my deeds to croffe,
Ioyne with the fpight of fortune, make me bow,
And doe not drop in for an after loffe :
Ah doe not, when my heart hath fcapte this forrow,
Come in the rereward of a conquerd woe,
Giue not a windy night a rainie morrow,
To linger out a purpofd ouer-throw.
If thou wilt leaue me, do not leaue me laft,
When other pettie griefes haue done their fpight,
But in the onfet come, fo ftall I tafte
At firft the very worft of fortunes might.
    And other ftraines of woe, which now feeme woe,
    Compar'd with loffe of thee, will not feeme fo.

91

SOme glory in their birth, fome in their skill,
    Some in their wealth, fome in their bodies force,
Some in their garments though new-fangled ill :
Some in their Hawkes and Hounds, fome in their Horfe.
And euery humor hath his adiunct pleafure,
Wherein it findes a ioy aboue the reft,
But thefe perticulers are not my meafure,
All thefe I better in one generall beft.
                                        Thy

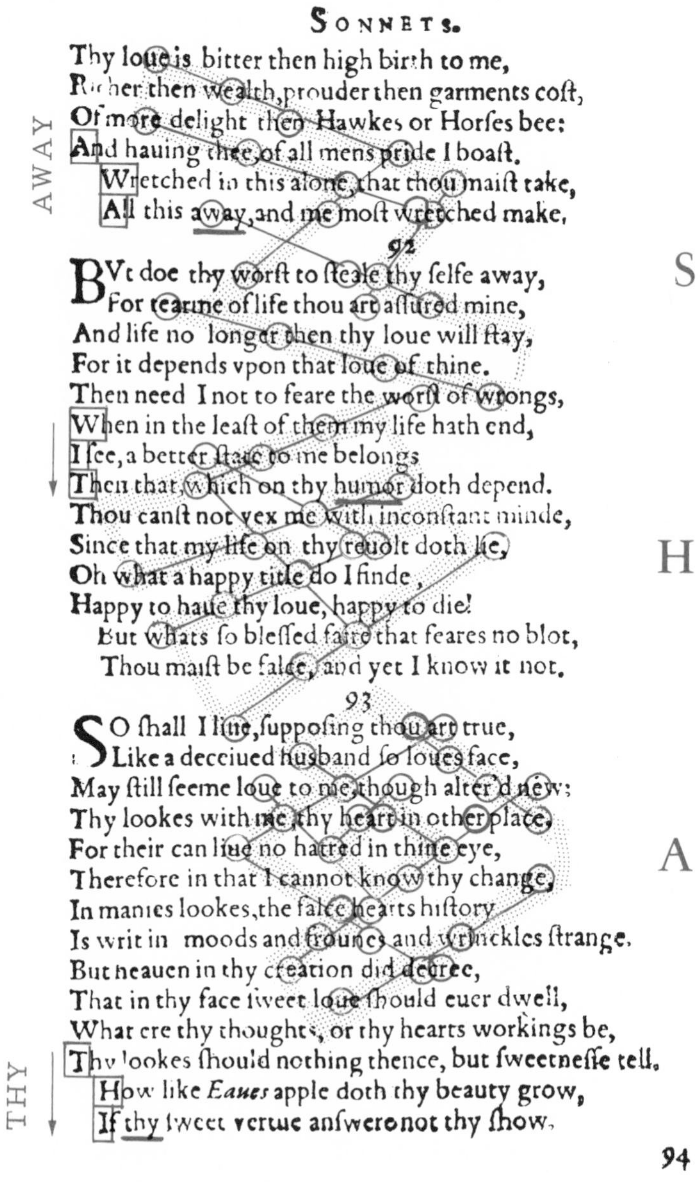

SONNETS.

Thy loue is bitter then high birth to me,
Richer then wealth,prouder then garments coſt,
Of more delight then Hawkes or Horſes bee:
And hauing thee,of all mens pride I boaſt.
  Wretched in this alone,that thou maiſt take,
  All this away,and me moſt wretched make.

AWAY

92

BVt doe thy worſt to ſteale thy ſelfe away,
  For tearme of life thou art aſſured mine,
And life no longer then thy loue will ſtay,
For it depends vpon that loue of thine.
Then need I not to feare the worſt of wrongs,
When in the leaſt of them my life hath end,
I ſee,a better ſtate to me belongs
Then that,which on thy humor doth depend.
Thou canſt not vex me with inconſtant minde,
Since that my life on thy reuolt doth lie,
Oh what a happy title do I finde,
Happy to haue thy loue,happy to die!
  But whats ſo bleſſed faire that feares no blot,
  Thou maiſt be falſe,and yet I know it not.

S

H

93

SO ſhall I liue,ſuppoſing thou art true,
  Like a deceiued husband ſo loues face,
May ſtill ſeeme loue to me though alter'd new:
Thy lookes with me,thy heart in other place,
For their can liue no hatred in thine eye,
Therefore in that I cannot know thy change.
In manies lookes,the falſe hearts hiſtory
Is writ in moods and frounes and wrinkles ſtrange.
But heauen in thy creation did decree,
That in thy face ſweet loue ſhould euer dwell,
What ere thy thoughts,or thy hearts workings be,
Thy lookes ſhould nothing thence,but ſweetneſſe tell.
  How like Eaues apple doth thy beauty grow,
  If thy ſweet vertue anſwere not thy ſhow.

A

THY

94

Here the signal WIT lacks significance. Perhaps the author hoped to squeeze four letters on this page but finally contented himself with three.

Thy loue is bitter then high birth to me,
Richer then wealth, prouder then garments coft,
Of more delight then Hawkes or Horfes bee :
And hauing thee, of all mens pride I boaft.
  Wretched in this alone, that thou maift take,
  All this away, and me moft wretched make.

92

BVt doe thy worft to fteale thy felfe away,
  For tearme of life thou art affured mine,
And life no longer then thy loue will ftay,
For it depends vpon that loue of thine.
Then need I not to feare the worft of wrongs,
When in the leaft of them my life hath end,
I fee, a better ftate to me belongs
Then that, which on thy humor doth depend.
Thou canft not vex me with inconftant minde,
Since that my life on thy reuolt doth lie,
Oh what a happy title do I finde,
Happy to haue thy loue, happy to die !
  But whats fo bleffed faire that feares no blot,
  Thou maift be falce, and yet I know it not.

93

SO fhall I liue, fuppofing thou art true,
  Like a deceiued husband, fo loues face,
May ftill feeme loue to me, though alter'd new :
Thy lookes with me, thy heart in other place.
For their can liue no hatred in thine eye,
Therefore in that I cannot know thy change,
In manies lookes, the falce hearts hiftory
Is writ in moods and frounes and wrinckles ftrange,
But heauen in thy creation did decree,
That in thy face fweet loue fhould euer dwell,
What ere thy thoughts, or thy hearts workings be,
Thy lookes fhould nothing thence, but fweetneffe tell.
  How like *Eaues* apple doth thy beauty grow,
  If thy fweet vertue anfwere not thy fhow.

94

THey that haue powre to hurt,and will doe none,
That doe not do the thing,they moſt do ſhowe,
Who mouing others,are themſelues as ſtone,
Vnmooued,coulde,and to temptation ſlow:
They rightly do inherit heauens graces,
And husband natures ritches from expence,
They are the Lords and owners of their faces,
Others,but ſtewards of their excellence:
The ſommers flowre is to the ſommer ſweet,
Though to it ſelfe,it onely liue and die,
But if that flowre with baſe infection meete,
The baſeſt weed out-braues his dignity:
   For ſweeteſt things turne ſowreſt by their deedes,
   Lillies that feſter,ſmell far worſe then weeds.

95

HOw ſweet and louely doſt thou make the ſhame,
Which like a canker in the fragrant Roſe,
Doth ſpot the beautie of thy budding name?
Oh in what ſweets doeſt thou thy ſinnes incloſe!
That tongue that tells the ſtory of thy daies,
(Making laſciuious comments on thy ſport)
Cannot diſpraiſe,but in a kinde of praiſe,
Naming thy name,bleſſes an ill report.
Oh what a manſion haue thoſe vices got,
Which for their habitation choſe out thee,
Where beauties vaile doth couer euery blot,
And all things turnes to faire that eies can ſee!
   Take heed(deare heart)of this large priuiledge,
   The hardeſt knife ill vſd doth looſe his edge.

96

SOme ſay thy fault is youth,ſome wantoneſſe,
Some ſay thy grace is youth and gentle ſport,
Both grace and faults are lou'd of more and leſſe:
Thou makſt faults graces,that to thee reſort:
As on the finger of a throned Queene,

The

This is one of the less inspired pages of block letters. Every author will have his off days. Nevertheless, the system has been faithfully followed to produce these mediocre letters.

94

THey that haue powre to hurt, and will doe none,
  That doe not do the thing, they moſt do ſhowe,
Who mouing others, are themſelues as ſtone,
Vnmooued, could, and to temptation ſlow :
They rightly do inherrit heauens graces,
And husband natures ritches from expence,
They are the Lords and owners of their faces,
Others, but ſtewards of their excellence :
The ſommers flowre is to the ſommer ſweet,
Though to it ſelfe, it onely liue and die,
But if that flowre with baſe infection meete,
The baſeſt weed out-braues his dignity :
    For ſweeteſt things turne ſowreſt by their deedes,
    Lillies that feſter, ſmell far worſe then weeds.

95

HOw ſweet and louely doſt thou make the ſhame,
  Which like a canker in the fragrant Roſe,
Doth ſpot the beautie of thy budding name ?
Oh in what ſweets doeſt thou thy ſinnes incloſe !
That tongue that tells the ſtory of thy daies,
(Making laſciuious comments on thy ſport)
Cannot diſpraiſe, but in a kinde of praiſe,
Naming thy name, bleſſes an ill report.
Oh what a manſion haue thoſe vices got,
Which for their habitation choſe out thee,
Where beauties vaile doth couer euery blot,
And all things turnes to faire, that eies can ſee !
    Take heed (deare heart) of this large priuiledge,
    The hardeſt knife ill vſ'd doth looſe his edge.

96

SOme ſay thy fault is youth, ſome wantoneſſe,
  Some ſay thy grace is youth and gentle ſport,
Both grace and faults are lou'd of more and leſſe :
Thou makſt faults graces, that to thee reſort :
As on the finger of a throned Queene,

                                        The

108

SONNETS.

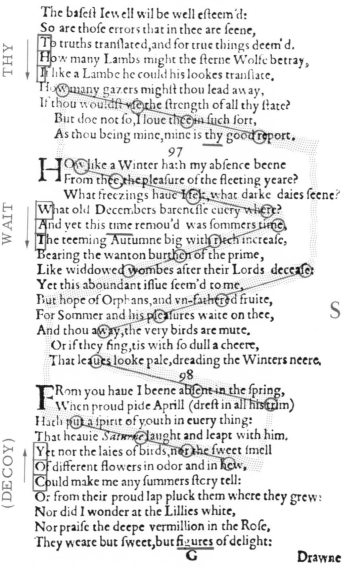

The basest Iewell wil be well esteem'd:
So are those errors that in thee are seene,
To truths translated,and for true things deem'd.
How many Lambs might the sterne Wolfe betray,
If like a Lambe he could his lookes translate.
How many gazers might thou lead away,
If thou wouldst vse the strength of all thy state?
　But doe not so,I loue thee in such sort,
　As thou being mine,mine is thy good report.

THY

97

HOw like a Winter hath my absence beene
From thee,the pleasure of the fleeting yeare?
　What freezings haue I felt,what darke daies seene?
What old Decembers barenesse euery where?
And yet this time remou'd was sommers time,
The teeming Autumne big with ritch increase,
Bearing the wanton burthen of the prime,
Like widdowed wombes after their Lords decease:
Yet this aboundant issue seem'd to me,
But hope of Orphans,and vn-fathered fruite,
For Sommer and his pleasures waite on thee,
And thou away,the very birds are mute.
　Or if they sing,tis with so dull a cheere,
　That leaues looke pale,dreading the Winters neere.

WAIT

S

98

FRom you haue I beene absent in the spring,
When proud pide Aprill (drest in all his trim)
Hath put a spirit of youth in euery thing:
That heauie Saturne laught and leapt with him.
Yet nor the laies of birds,nor the sweet smell
Of different flowers in odor and in hew,
Could make me any summers story tell:
Or from their proud lap pluck them where they grew:
Nor did I wonder at the Lillies white,
Nor praise the deepe vermillion in the Rose,
They weare but sweet,but figures of delight:

(DECOY)

G　　　　　　　　　Drawne

Here although the block letter S extends into three Sonnets
and is the only letter on the page, he has provided a signal and
link in each verse.

The baſeſt Iewell wil be well eſteemed :
So are thoſe errors that in thee are ſeene,
To truths tranſlated, and for true things deem'd.
How many Lambs might the ſterne Wolfe betray,
If like a Lambe he could his lookes tranſlate.
How many gazers mighſt thou lead away,
If thou wouldſt vſe the ſtrength of all thy ſtate ?
   But doe not ſo, I loue thee in ſuch ſort,
   As thou being mine, mine is thy good report.

97

HOw like a Winter hath my abſence beene
  From thee, the pleaſure of the fleeting yeare ?
   What freezings haue I felt, what darke daies ſeene ?
What old Decembers bareneſſe euery where ?
And yet this time remou'd was ſommers time,
The teeming Autumne big with ritch increaſe,
Bearing the wanton burthen of the prime,
Like widdowed wombes after their Lords deceaſe :
Yet this aboundant iſſue ſeem'd to me,
But hope of Orphans, and vn-fathered fruite,
For Sommer and his pleaſures waite on thee,
And thou away, the very birds are mute.
   Or if they ſing, tis with ſo dull a cheere,
   That leaues looke pale, dreading the Winters neere.

98

FRom you haue I beene abſent in the ſpring,
  When proud pide Aprill (dreſt in all his trim)
Hath put a ſpirit of youth in euery thing :
That heauie *Saturne* laught and leapt with him.
Yet nor the laies of birds, nor the ſweet ſmell
Of different flowers in odor and in hew,
Could make me any ſummers ſtory tell :
Or from their proud lap pluck them where they grew :
Nor did I wonder at the Lillies white,
Nor praiſe the deepe vermillion in the Roſe,
They weare but ſweet, but figures of delight :
             G   Drawne

110

Drawn after you, you patterne of all thofe.
  Yet feem'd it Winter ftill, and you away,
  As with your fhaddow I with thefe did play.

99

THe forward violet thus did I chide,
    Sweet theefe whence didft thou fteale thy fweet that
If not from my loues breath, the purple pride,   (fmels
Which on thy foft cheeke for complexion dwells?
In my loues veines thou haft too grofely died,
The Lillie I condemned for thy hand,
And buds of marierom had ftolne thy haire,
The Rofes fearefully on thornes did ftand,
Our blufhing fhame an other white difpaire:
A third nor red, nor white, had ftolne of both,
And to his robbry had annext thy breath,
But for his theft in pride of all his growth
A vengfull canker eate him vp to death.
    More flowers I noted, yet I none could fee,
    But fweet, or culler it had ftolne from thee.

100

VVHere art thou Mufe that thou forgetft fo long,
      To fpeake of that which giues thee all thy might?
Spendft thou thy furie on fome worthleffe fonge,
Darkning thy powre to lend bafe fubiects light.
Returne forgetfull Mufe, and ftraight redeeme,
In gentle numbers time fo idely fpent,
Sing to the eare that doth thy laies efteeme,
And giues thy pen both skill and argument.
Rife refty Mufe, my loues fweet face furuay,
If time haue any wrincle grauen there,
If any, be a *Satire* to decay,
And make times fpoiles difpifed euery where.
    Giue my loue fame fafter then time waftes life,
    So thou preuenft his fieth, and crooked knife.

101

OH truant Mufe what fhalbe thy amends,

                                                    For

P

E

RISE

The signal WIT comes up again and this concludes a five page
sequence reading WIT, WIT, WAT, WAT, WIT. Possibly
this pattern was thus placed as a flag to aid initial discovery
of the system.

Drawne after you, you patterne of all thofe.
   Yet feem'd it Winter ftill, and you away,
   As with your fhaddow I with thefe did play.

99

THe forward violet thus did I chide,
   Sweet theefe whence didft thou fteale thy fweet that
If not from my loues breath, the purple pride,   (fmels
Which on thy foft cheeke for complexion dwells ?
In my loues veines thou haft too grofely died,
The Lillie I condemned for thy hand,
And buds of marierom had ftolne thy haire,
The Rofes fearefully on thornes did ftand,
Our blufhing fhame, an other white difpaire :
A third nor red, nor white, had ftolne of both,
And to his robbry had annext thy breath,
But for his theft in pride of all his growth
A vengfull canker eate him vp to death.
   More flowers I noted, yet I none could fee,
   But fweet, or culler it had ftolne from thee.

100

VVHere art thou Mufe that thou forgetft fo long,
   To fpeake of that which giues thee all thy might ?
Spendft thou thy furie on fome worthleffe fonge,
Darkning thy powre to lend bafe fubiects light,
Returne forgetfull Mufe, and ftraight redeeme,
In gentle numbers time fo idely fpent,
Sing to the eare that doth thy laies efteeme,
And giues thy pen both skill and argument.
Rife refty Mufe, my loues fweet face furuay,
If time haue any wrincle grauen there,
If any, be a *Satire* to decay,
And make times fpoiles difpifed euery where.
   Giue my loue fame fafter then time wafts life,
   So thou preuenft his fieth, and crooked knife.

101

OH truant Mufe what fhalbe thy amends,

                                     For

SONNETS.

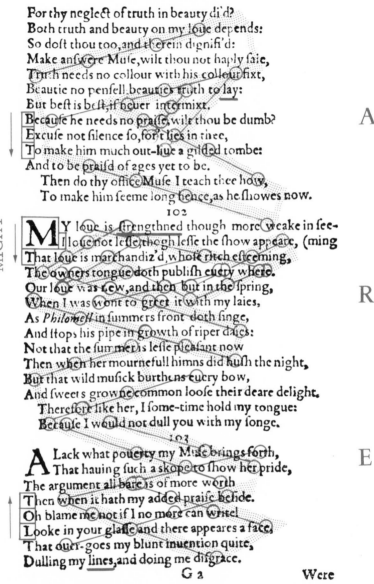

For thy neglect of truth in beauty di'd?
Both truth and beauty on my loue depends:
So dost thou too,and therein dignifi'd:
Make answere Muse,wilt thou not haply saie,
Truth needs no collour with his collour fixt,
Beautie no pensell,beauties truth to lay:
But best is best,if neuer intermixt.
Because he needs no praise,wilt thou be dumb?
Excuse not silence so,for't lies in thee,
To make him much out-liue a gilded tombe:
And to be praisd of ages yet to be.
　　Then do thy office Muse I teach thee how,
　　To make him seeme long hence,as he showes now.

102

MY loue is strengthned though more weake in see-
I loue not lesse,though lesse the show appeare, (ming
That loue is marchandiz'd,whose ritch esteeming,
The owners tongue doth publish euery where.
Our loue was new,and then but in the spring,
When I was wont to greet it with my laies,
As *Philomell* in summers front doth singe,
And stops his pipe in growth of riper daies:
Not that the summer is lesse pleasant now
Then when her mournefull himns did hush the night,
But that wild musick burthens euery bow,
And sweets grown common loose their deare delight.
　　Therefore like her, I some-time hold my tongue:
　　Because I would not dull you with my songe.

103

ALack what pouerty my Muse brings forth,
That hauing such a skope to show her pride,
The argument all bare is of more worth
Then when it hath my added praise beside.
Oh blame me not if I no more can write!
Looke in your glasse and there appeares a face,
That ouer-goes my blunt inuention quite,
Dulling my lines,and doing me disgrace.

G 2　　　　　　　　Were

LOT associates with "lines" through its biblical meaning when a father divided his land to his sons by throwing a stone in a given direction to dilineate a boundary line. See Psalm 16: 5 & 6.

For thy neglect of truth in beauty di'd?
Both truth and beauty on my loue depends :
So doft thou too, and therein dignifi'd :
Make anfwere Mufe, wilt thou not haply faie,
Truth needs no collour with his collour fixt,
Beautie no penfell, beauties truth to lay :
But beft is beft, if neuer intermixt.
Becaufe he needs no praife, wilt thou be dumb ?
Excufe not filence fo, for't lies in thee,
To make him much out-liue a gilded tombe :
And to be praifd of ages yet to be.
    Then do thy office Mufe, I teach thee how,
    To make him feeme long hence, as he fhowes now.

102

MY loue is ftrengthned though more weake in fee-
  I loue not leffe, thogh leffe the fhow appeare, (ming
That loue is marchandiz'd, whofe ritch efteeming,
The owners tongue doth publifh euery where.
Our loue was new, and then but in the fpring,
When I was wont to greet it with my laies,
As *Philomell* in fummers front doth finge,
And ftops his pipe in growth of riper daies :
Not that the fummer is leffe pleafant now
Then when her mournefull himns did hufh the night,
But that wild mufick burthens euery bow,
And fweets growne common loofe their deare delight.
    Therefore like her, I fome-time held my tongue :
    Becaufe I would not dull you with my fonge.

103

A Lack what pouerty my Mufe brings forth,
  That hauing fuch a skope to fhow her pride,
The argument all bare is of more worth
Then when it hath my added praife befide.
Oh blame me not if I no more can write !
Looke in your glaffe and there appeares a face,
That ouer-goes my blunt inuention quite,
Dulling my lines, and doing me difgrace.
             G 2   Were

114

SHAKE-SPEARES.

Were it not finfull then ftriuing to mend,
To marre the fubiect that before was well,
For to no other paffe my verfes tend,
Then of your graces and your gifts to tell.
    And more,much more then in my verfe can fit,
    Your owne glaffe fhowes you,when you looke in it

104

TO me faire friend you neuer can be old,
  For as you were when firft your eye I eyde,
Such feemes your beautie ftill:Three Winters colde,
Haue from the forrefts fhooke three fummers pride,
Three beautious fprings to yellow *Autumne* turn'd,
In proceffe of the feafons haue I feene,
Three Aprill perfumes in three hot Iunes burn'd,
Since firft I faw you frefh which yet are greene.
Ah yet doth beauty like a Dyall hand,
Steale from his figure,and no pace perceiu'd,
So your fweete hew,which me thinkes ftill doth ftand
Hath motion,and mine eye may be deceaued.
    For feare of which,heare this thou age vnbred,
    Ere you were borne was beauties fummer dead.

O

X

105

LEt not my loue be cal'd Idolatrie,
  Nor my beloued as an Idoll fhow,
Since all alike my fongs and praifes be
To one,of one,ftill fuch,and euer fo.
Kinde is my loue to day,to morrow kinde,
Still conftant in a wondrous excellence,
Therefore my verfe to conftancie confin'de,
One thing expreffing,leaues out difference.
Faire,kinde,and true,is all my argument,
Faire,kinde and true,varrying to other words,
And in this change is my inuention fpent,
Three theams in one,which wondrous fcope affords.
    Faire,kinde,and true,haue often liu'd alone.
    Which three till now,neuer kept feate in one.

F

When

After the perfectly symmetrical X at the top as a spacer, the
author proceeds to spell OXFORD in FAT letters and again
starts out with a high standard of letter contours.

Sonnet 104 is a tribute to Elizabeth Trentham's figure written
three years after their marriage in 1590 or 1591. The marginal
signals leave no doubt about the subject matter of this verse.

Were it not finfull then ftriuing to mend,
To marre the fubiect that before was well,
For to no other paffe my verfes tend,
Then of your graces and your gifts to tell.
   And more, much more then in my verfe can fit,
   Your owne glaffe fhowes you, when you looke in it.

104

TO me faire friend you neuer can be old,
  For as you were when firft your eye I eyde,
Such feemes your beautie ftill : Three Winters colde,
Haue from the forrefts fhooke three fummers pride,
Three beautious fprings to yellow *Autumne* turn'd,
In proceffe of the feafons haue I feene,
Three Aprill perfumes in three hot Iunes burn'd,
Since firft I faw you frefh which yet are greene.
Ah yet doth beauty like a Dyall hand,
Steale from his figure, and no pace perceiu'd,
So your fweete hew, which me thinkes ftill doth ftand
Hath motion, and mine eye may be deceaued.
   For feare of which, heare this thou age vnbred,
   Ere you were borne was beauties fummer dead.

105

LEt not my loue be cal'd Idolatrie,
  Nor my beloued as an Idoll fhow,
Since all alike my fongs and praifes be
To-one, of one, ftill fuch, and euer fo.
Kinde is my loue to day, to morrow kinde,
Still conftant in a wondrous excellence,
Therefore my verfe to conftancie confin'de,
One thing expreffing, leaues out difference.
Faire, kinde, and true, is all my argument,
Faire, kinde and true, varrying to other words,
And in this change is my inuention fpent,
Three theams in one, which wondrous fcope affords.
   Faire, kinde, and true, haue often liu'd alone.
   Which three till now, neuer kept feate in one.

                       When

SONNETS.

106

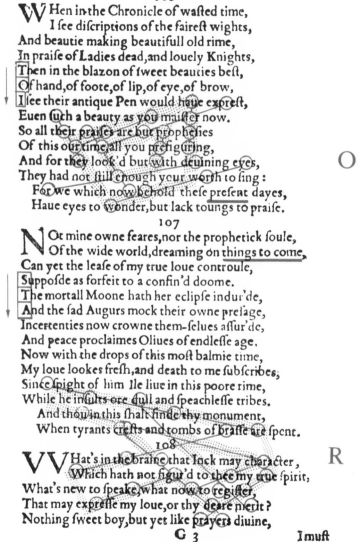

WHen in the Chronicle of wasted time,
    I see discriptions of the fairest wights,
And beautie making beautifull old rime,
In praise of Ladies dead, and louely Knights,
Then in the blazon of sweet beauties best,
Of hand, of foote, of lip, of eye, of brow,
I see their antique Pen would haue exprest,
Euen such a beauty as you maister now.
So all their praises are but prophesies
Of this our time, all you prefiguring,
And for they look'd but with deuining eyes,
They had not still enough your worth to sing:
    For we which now behold these present dayes,
    Haue eyes to wonder, but lack toungs to praise.

107

NOt mine owne feares, nor the prophetick soule,
    Of the wide world, dreaming on things to come,
Can yet the lease of my true loue controule,
Supposde as forfeit to a confin'd doome.
The mortall Moone hath her eclipse indur'de,
And the sad Augurs mock their owne presage,
Incertenties now crowne them-selues assur'de,
And peace proclaimes Oliues of endlesse age.
Now with the drops of this most balmie time,
My loue lookes fresh, and death to me subscribes,
Since spight of him Ile liue in this poore rime,
While he insults ore dull and speachlesse tribes.
    And thou in this shalt finde thy monument,
    When tyrants crests and tombs of brasse are spent.

108

WHat's in the braine that Inck may character,
    Which hath not figur'd to thee my true spirit,
What's new to speake, what now to register,
That may expresse my loue, or thy deare merit?
Nothing sweet boy, but yet like prayers diuine,

                    G 3   I must

Again the standards are slipping, this time the author is taking
liberties with the acrostics themselves such as by skipping a
line or two.

106

WHen in the Chronicle of wasted time,
  I see discriptions of the fairest wights,
And beautie making beautifull old rime,
In praise of Ladies dead, and louely Knights,
Then in the blazon of sweet beauties best,
Of hand, of foote, of lip, of eye, of brow,
I see their antique Pen would haue exprest,
Euen such a beauty as you maister now.
So all their praises are but prophesies
Of this our time, all you prefiguring,
And for they look'd but with deuining eyes,
They had not still enough your worth to sing :
    For we which now behold these present dayes,
    Haue eyes to wonder, but lack toungs to praise.

107

NOt mine owne feares, nor the prophetick soule,
  Of the wide world, dreaming on things to come,
Can yet the lease of my true loue controule,
Suppolde as forfeit to a confin'd doome.
The mortall Moone hath her eclipse indur'de,
And the sad Augurs mock their owne presage,
Incertenties now crowne them-selues assur'de,
And peace proclaimes Oliues of endlesse age.
Now with the drops of this most balmie time,
My loue lookes fresh, and death to me subscribes,
Since spight of him Ile liue in this poore rime,
While he insults ore dull and speachlesse tribes.
    And thou in this shalt finde thy monument,
    When tyrants crests and tombs of brasse are spent.

108

VVHat's in the braine that Inck may character,
  Which hath not figur'd to thee my true spirit,
What's new to speake, what now to register,
That may expresse my loue, or thy deare merit ?
Nothing sweet boy, but yet like prayers diuine,
                    G 3   I must

SHAKE-SPEARES.

I muſt each day ſay ore the very ſame,
Counting no old thing old,thou mine,I thine,
Euen as when firſt I hallowed thy faire name.
So that eternall loue in loues freſh caſe,
Waighes not the duſt and iniury of age,
Nor giues to neceſſary wrinckles place,
But makes antiquitie for aye his page,
    Finding the firſt conceit of loue there bred,
    Where time and outward forme would ſhew it dead,

109

O Neuer ſay that I was falſe of heart,
    Though abſence ſeem'd my flame to quallifie,
As eaſie might I from my ſelfe depart,
As from my ſoule which in thy breſt doth lye :
That is my home of loue, if I haue rang'd,
Like him that trauels I returne againe,
Iuſt to the time, not with the time exchang'd,
So that my ſelfe bring water for my ſtaine,
Neuer beleeue though in my nature raign'd,
All frailties that beſiege all kindes of blood,
That it could ſo prepoſterouſlie be ſtain'd,
To leaue for nothing all thy ſumme of good :
    For nothing this wide Vniuerſe I call,
    Saue thou my Roſe,in it thou art my all.

110

A Las 'tis true,I haue gone here and there,
    And made my ſelfe a motley to the view,
Gor'd mine own thoughts, ſold cheap what is moſt deare,
Made old offences of affections new.
Moſt true it is,that I haue lookt on truth
Aſconce and ſtrangely: But by all aboue,
Theſe blenches gaue my heart an other youth,
And worſe eſſaies prou'd thee my beſt of loue,
Now all is done,haue what ſhall haue no end,
Mine appetite I neuer more will grin'de
On newer proofe,to trie an older friend,
A God in loue,to whom I am confin'd.

Then

The spacer pattern after OXFORD is a well formed V and a
pair of perfect X's. The signal GAA links to "a motley" the
costume of the court jester or fool.

I muſt each day ſay ore the very ſame,
Counting no old thing old, thou mine, I thine,
Euen as when firſt I hallowed thy faire name,
So that eternall loue in loues freſh caſe,
Waighes not the duſt and iniury of age.
Nor giues to neceſſary wrinckles place,
But makes antiquitie for aye his page.
   Finding the firſt conceit of loue there bred,
   Where time and outward forme would ſhew it dead.

109

O Neuer ſay that I was falſe of heart,
   Though abſence feem'd my flame to quallifie,
As eaſie might I from my ſelfe depart,
As from my ſoule which in thy breſt doth lye :
That is my home of loue, if I haue rang'd,
Like him that trauels I returne againe,
Iuſt to the time, not with the time exchang'd,
So that my ſelfe bring water for my ſtaine,
Neuer beleeue though in my nature raign'd,
All frailties that beſiege all kindes of blood,
That it could ſo prepoſterouſlie be ſtain'd,
To leaue for nothing all thy ſumme of good :
   For nothing this wide Vniuerſe I call,
   Saue thou my Roſe, in it thou art my all.

110

A Las 'tis true, I haue gone here and there,
   And made my ſelfe a motley to the view,
Gor'd mine own thoughts, ſold cheap what is moſt deare,
Made old offences of affections new.
Moſt true it is, that I haue lookt on truth
Aſconce and ſtrangely : But by all aboue,
Theſe blenches gaue my heart an other youth,
And worſe eſſaies prou'd thee my beſt of loue,
Now all is done, haue what ſhall haue no end,
Mine appetite I neuer more will grin'de
On newer proofe, to trie an older friend,
A God in loue, to whom I am confin'd.

                        Then

120

SONNETS.

Then giue me welcome next my heauen the beſt,
Euen to thy pure and moſt moſt louing breſt.

111

O For my ſake doe you wiſh fortune chide,
   The guiltie goddeſſe of my harmfull deeds,
That did not better for my life prouide,
Then publick meanes which publick manners breeds.
Thence comes it that my name receiues a brand,
And almoſt thence my nature is ſubdu'd
To what it workes in, like the Dyers hand,
Pitty me then, and wiſh I were renu'de,
Whilſt like a willing pacient I will drinke,
Potions of Eyſell gainſt my ſtrong infection,
No bitterneſſe that I will bitter thinke,
Nor double pennance to correct correction.
   Pittie me then deare friend, and I aſſure yee,
   Euen that your pittie is enough to cure mee.

PUP

O

X

112

YOur loue and pittie doth th'impreſſion fill,
   Which vulgar ſcandall ſtampt vpon my brow,
For what care I who calles me well or ill,
So you ore-greene my bad, my good alow?
You are my All the world, and I muſt ſtriue,
To know my ſhames and praiſes from your tounge,
None elſe to me, nor I to none aliue,
That my ſteel'd ſence or changes right or wrong,
In ſo profound Abiſme I throw all care
Of others voyces, that my Adders ſence,
To cryttick and to flatterer ſtopped are:
Marke how with my neglect I doe diſpence.
   You are ſo ſtrongly in my purpoſe bred,
   That all the world beſides me thinkes y'are dead.

SIGHT

F

113

SInce I left you, mine eye is in my minde,
   And that which gouernes me to goe about,
Doth part his function, and is partly blind,

MIGHT

Seemes

Here begins another OXFORD with such a tiny beginning
letter that possibly the signal PUP is meant to refer to it.

Then giue me welcome, next my heauen the beſt,
Euen to thy pure and moſt moſt louing breſt.

III

O For my ſake doe you wiſh fortune chide,
   The guiltie goddeſſe of my harmfull deeds,
That did not better for my life prouide,
Then publick meanes which publick manners breeds.
Thence comes it that my name receiues a brand,
And almoſt thence my nature is ſubdu'd
To what it workes in, like the Dyers hand,
Pitty me then, and wiſh I were renu'de,
Whilſt like a willing pacient I will drinke,
Potions of Eyſell gainſt my ſtrong infection,
No bitterneſſe that I will bitter thinke,
Nor double pennance to correct correction.
  Pittie me then deare friend, and I aſſure yee,
  Euen that your pittie is enough to cure mee.

112

Y Our loue and pittie doth th'impreſſion fill,
   Which vulgar ſcandall ſtampt vpon my brow,
For what care I who calles me well or ill,
So you ore-greene my bad, my good alow?
You are my All the world, and I muſt ſtriue,
To know my ſhames and praiſes from your tounge,
None elſe to me, nor I to none aliue,
That my ſteel'd ſence or changes right or wrong,
In ſo profound *Abiſme* I throw all care
Of others voyces, that my Adders ſence,
To cryttick and to flatterer ſtopped are :
Marke how with my neglect I doe diſpence.
  You are ſo ſtrongly in my purpoſe bred,
  That all the world beſides me thinkes y'are dead.

113

S Ince I left you, mine eye is in my minde,
  And that which gouernes me to goe about,
Doth part his function, and is partly blind,

Seemes

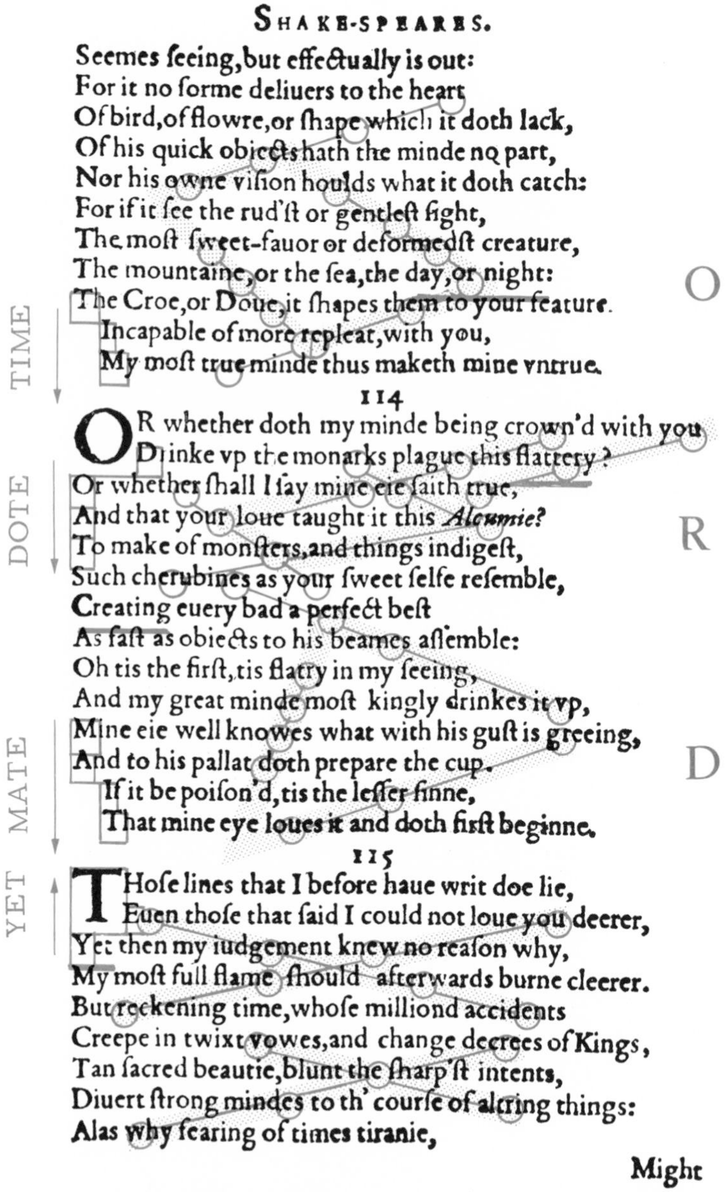
TIME
DOTE
MATE
YET
O
R
D

SHAKE-SPEARES.

Seemes ſeeing, but effectually is out:
For it no forme deliuers to the heart
Of bird, of flowre, or ſhape which it doth lack,
Of his quick obiects hath the minde no part,
Nor his owne viſion houlds what it doth catch:
For if it ſee the rud'ſt or gentleſt ſight,
The moſt ſweet-fauor or deformedſt creature,
The mountaine, or the ſea, the day, or night:
The Croe, or Doue, it ſhapes them to your feature.
Incapable of more repleat, with you,
My moſt true minde thus maketh mine vntrue.

114

OR whether doth my minde being crown'd with you
Drinke vp the monarks plague this flattery?
Or whether ſhall I ſay mine eie ſaith true,
And that your loue taught it this *Alcumie?*
To make of monſters, and things indigeſt,
Such cherubines as your ſweet ſelfe reſemble,
Creating euery bad a perfect beſt
As faſt as obiects to his beames aſſemble:
Oh tis the firſt, tis flatry in my ſeeing,
And my great minde moſt kingly drinkes it vp,
Mine eie well knowes what with his guſt is greeing,
And to his pallat doth prepare the cup.
If it be poiſon'd, tis the leſſer ſinne,
That mine eye loues it and doth firſt beginne.

115

THoſe lines that I before haue writ doe lie,
Euen thoſe that ſaid I could not loue you deerer,
Yet then my iudgement knew no reaſon why,
My moſt full flame ſhould afterwards burne cleerer.
But reckening time, whoſe milliond accidents
Creepe in twixt vowes, and change decrees of Kings,
Tan ſacred beautie, blunt the ſharp'ſt intents,
Diuert ſtrong mindes to th' courſe of altring things:
Alas why fearing of times tiranie,

Might

As this OXFORD is completed, the spacer is a simple pair of X's.

Another instance of deliberate mis-spelling for the purpose of supplying a needed acrostic letter appears at line 9 of Sonnet 114 in the word "flatry." He knows better for in line 2 he spells it "flattery."

Seemes feeing, but effectually is out :
For it no forme deliuers to the heart
Of bird, of flowre, or fhape which it doth lack,
Of his quick obiects hath the minde no part,
Nor his owne vifion houlds what it doth catch :
For if it fee the rud'ft or gentleft fight,
The moft fweet-fauor or deformedft creature,
The mountaine, or the fea, the day, or night :
The Croe, or Doue, it fhapes them to your feature.
   Incapable of more repleat, with you,
   My moft true minde thus maketh mine vntrue.

114

OR whether doth my minde being crown'd with you
  Drinke vp the monarks plague this flattery ?
Or whether fhall I fay mine eie faith true,
And that your loue taught it this *Alcumie ?*
To make of monfters, and things indigeft,
Such cherubines as your fweet felfe refemble,
Creating euery bad a perfect beft
As faft as obiects to his beames affemble :
Oh tis the firft, tis flatry in my feeing,
And my great minde moft kingly drinkes it vp,
Mine eie well knowes what with his guft is greeing,
And to his pallat doth prepare the cup.
   If it be poifon'd, tis the leffer finne,
   That mine eye loues it and doth firft beginne.

115

THofe lines that I before haue writ doe lie,
  Euen thofe that faid I could not loue you deerer,
Yet then my iugdement knew no reafon why,
My moft full flame fhould afterwards burne cleerer.
But reckening time, whofe milliond accidents
Creepe in twixt vowes, and change decrees of Kings,
Tan facred beautie, blunt the fharp'ft intents,
Diuert ftronge mindes to th' courfe of altring things :
Alas why fearing of times tiranie,
                  Might

SONNETS.

MUCK

Might I not then fay now I loue you beſt,
When I was certaine ore in-certainty,
Crowning the preſent, doubting of the reſt:
 Loue is a Babe, then might I not fay ſo
 To giue full growth to that which ſtill doth grow.

119 116

LEt me not to the marriage of true mindes
 Admit impediments, loue is not loue
Which alters when it alteration findes,
Or bends with the remouer to remoue.
O no, it is an euer fixed marke
That lookes on tempeſts and is neuer ſhaken;
It is the ſtar to euery wandring barke,
Whoſe worths vnknowne, although his higth be taken.
Lou's not Times foole, though roſie lips and cheeks
Within his bending ſickles compaſſe come,
Loue alters not with his breefe houres and weekes,
But beares it out euen to the edge of doome:
 If this be error and vpon me proued,
 I neuer writ, nor no man euer loued.

117

ACcuſe me thus, that I haue ſcanted all,
 Wherein I ſhould your great deſerts repay,
Forgot vpon your deareſt loue to call,
Whereto al bonds do tie me day by day,
That I haue frequent binne with vnknown mindes,
And giuen to time your owne deare purchaſ'd right,
That I haue hoyſted ſaile to al the windes
Which ſhould tranſport me fartheſt from your ſight.
Booke both my wilfulneſſe and errors downe,
And on iuſt proofe ſurmiſe, accumilate,
Bring me within the leuel of your frowne,
But ſhoote not at me in your wakened hate:
 Since my appeale ſaies I did ſtriue to proue
 The conſtancy and virtue of your loue

TUB

H 118

Here begins the most amazing run of acrostics in the entire
series. WILLIAM SHAKESPEARE is spelled out in block
letters but instead of letting them appear in random orienta-
tions each letter is so positioned that it reads right-side-up by
turning the page so that the left-hand margin becomes the
base. Another deliberate mis-spelling occurs in line 5 of Sonnet 117 where the participle "been" is spelled as the noun
"binne" in order to link to TUB.

Might I not then fay now I loue you beſt,
When I was certaine ore in-certainty,
Crowning the prefent, doubting of the reſt :
    Loue is a Babe, then might J not fay fo
    To giue full growth to that which ſtill doth grow.

119   (116)

LEt me not to the marriage of true mindes
    Admit impediments, loue is not loue
Which alters when it alteration findes,
Or bends with the remouer to remoue.
O no, it is an euer fixed marke
That lookes on tempeſts and is neuer ſhaken ;
It is the ſtar to euery wandring barke,
Whofe worths vnknowne, although his higth be taken.
Lou's not Times foole, though rofie lips and cheeks
Within his bending fickles compaſſe come,
Loue alters not with his breefe houres and weekes,
But beares it out euen to the edge of doome :
    If this be error and vpon me proued,
    I neuer writ, nor no man euer loued.

117

ACcufe me thus, that I haue fcanted all,
    Wherein I ſhould your great deferts repay,
Forgot vpon your deareſt loue to call,
Whereto al bonds do tie me day by day,
That I haue frequent binne with vnknown mindes,
And giuen to time your owne deare purchaſ'd right,
That I haue hoyſted faile to al the windes
Which ſhould tranfport me fartheſt from your fight.
Booke both my wilfulneſſe and errors downe,
And on iuſt proofe furmife, accumilate,
Bring me within the leuel of your frowne,
But ſhoote not at me in your wakened hate :
    Since my appeale faies I did ſtriue to prooue
    The conſtancy and virtue of your loue

H   118

118

Like as to make our appetites more keene
With eager compounds we our pallat vrge,
As to preuent our malladies vnseene,
We sicken to shun sicknesse when we purge.
Euen so being full of your nere cloying sweetnesse,
To bitter sawces did I frame my feeding;
And sicke of wel-fare found a kind of meetnesse,
To be diseas'd ere that there was true needing.
Thus pollicie in loue t'anticipate
The ills that were, not grew to faults assured,
And brought to medicine a healthfull state
Which rancke of goodnesse would by ill be cured.
But thence I learne and find the lesson true,
Drugs poyson him that so fell sicke of you.

119

What potions haue I drunke of *Syren* teares
Distil'd from Lymbecks foule as hell within,
Applying feares to hopes, and hopes to feares,
Still loosing when I saw my selfe to win?
What wretched errors hath my heart committed,
Whilst it hath thought it selfe so blessed neuer?
How haue mine eies out of their Spheares bene fitted
In the distraction of this madding feuer?
O benefit of ill, now I find true
That better is, by euil still made better.
And ruin'd loue when it is built anew
Growes fairer then at first, more strong, far greater.
So I returne rebukt to my content,
And gaine by ills thrise more then I haue spent.

120

That you were once vnkind be-friends mee now,
And for that sorrow, which I then didde feele,
Needes must I vnder my transgression bow,
Vnlesse my Nerues were brasse or hammered steele.
For if you were by my vnkindnesse shaken

As

The reader was warned by the signal WIT on the preceding
page and another warning appears here in WAT.

118

Like as to make our appetites more keene
With eager compounds we our pallat vrge,
As to preuent our malladies vnfeene,
We ficken to fhun ficknefle when we purge.
Euen fo being full of your nere cloying fweetnefle,
To bitter fawces did I frame my feeding ;
And ficke of wel-fare found a kind of meetnefle,
To be difeaf'd ere that there was true needing.
Thus pollicie in loue t'anticipate
The ills that were, not grew to faults aflured,
And brought to medicine a healthfull ftate
Which rancke of goodnefle would by ill be cured.
    But thence I learne and find the leflon true,
    Drugs poyfon him that fo fell ficke of you.

119

WHat potions haue I drunke of *Syren* teares
Diftil'd from Lymbecks foule as hell within,
Applying feares to hopes, and hopes to feares,
Still loofing when I faw my felfe to win ?
What wretched errors hath my heart committed,
Whilft it hath thought it felfe fo blefled neuer ?
How haue mine eies out of their Spheares bene fitted
In the diftraction of this madding feuer ?
O benefit of ill, now I find true
That better is, by euil ftill made better.
And ruin'd loue when it is built anew
Growes fairer then at firft, more ftrong, far greater.
    So I returne rebukt to my content,
    And gaine by ills thrife more then I haue fpent.

120

THat you were once vnkind be-friends mee now,
And for that forrow , which I then didde feele,
Needes muft I vnder my tranfgreflion bow,
Vnlefle my Nerues were brafle or hammered fteele.
For if you were by my vnkindnefle fhaken

As

SONNETS.

As I by yours , y'haue paſt a hell of Time,
And I a tyrant haue no leaſure taken
To waigh how once I ſuffered in your crime.
O that our night of wo might haue remembred
My deepeſt ſence, how hard true ſorrow hits,
And ſoone to you, as you to me then tendred
The humble ſalue, which wounded boſomes fits!
  But that your treſpaſſe now becomes a fee,
  Mine ranſoms yours, and yours muſt ranſome mee.

MATE

M

121

TIS better to be vile then vile eſteemed,
  When not to be, receiues reproach of being,
And the iuſt pleaſure loſt, which is ſo deemed,
Not by our feeling, but by others ſeeing.
For why ſhould others falſe adulterat eyes
Giue ſalutation to my ſportiue blood?
Or on my frailties why are frailer ſpies,
Which in their wils count bad what I think good?
Noe, I am that I am, and they that leuell
At my abuſes, reckon vp their owne,
I may be ſtraight though they them-ſelues be beuel
By their rancke thoughtes, my deedes muſt not be ſhown
  Vnleſſe this generall euill they maintaine,
  All men are bad and in their badneſſe raigne.

S

122.

THy guift, thy tables, are within my braine
  Full charáfterd with laſting memory,
Which ſhall aboue that idle rancke remaine
Beyond all date euen to eternity.
Or at the leaſt, ſo long as braine and heart
Haue facultie by nature to ſubſiſt,
Till each to raz'd obliuion yeeld his part
Of thee, thy record neuer can be miſt:
  That poore retention could not ſo much hold,
  Nor need I tallies thy deare loue to skore,
  Therefore to giue them from me was I bold,

TOTE

H

H 2   To

That TOT is intended to be read TOTE linking with "tallies" is confirmed in Sonnet 141 where the same word links with "count." See also Sonnet 94 where TOT links with "stewards."

As I by yours , y'haue paſt a hell of Time,
And I a tyrant haue no leaſure taken
To waigh how once I ſuffered in your crime.
O that our night of wo might haue remembred
My deepeſt ſence, how hard true ſorrow hits,
And ſoone to you, as you to me then tendred
And humble ſalue, which wounded boſomes fits!
   But that your treſpaſſe now becomes a fee,
   Mine ranſoms yours, and yours muſt ranſome mee.

121

TIS better to be vile then vile eſteemed,
  When not to be, receiues reproach of being,
And the iuſt pleaſure loſt, which is ſo deemed,
Not by our feeling, but by others ſeeing.
For why ſhould others falſe adulterat eyes
Giue ſalutation to my ſportiue blood?
Or on my frailties why are frailer ſpies ;
Which in their wils count bad what I think good?
Noe, I am that I am, and they that leuell
At my abuſes, reckon vp their owne,
I may be ſtraight though they them-ſelues be beuel
By their rancke thoughtes, my deedes muſt not be ſhown
   Vnleſſe this general euill they maintaine,
   All men are bad and in their badneſſe raigne.

122.

TThy guift,, thy tables, are within my braine
  Full charaƈterd with laſting memory,
Which ſhall aboue that idle rancke remaine
Beyond all date euen to eternity.
Or at the leaſt, ſo long as braine and heart
Haue facultie by nature to ſubſiſt,
Til each to raz'd obliuion yeeld his part
Of thee, thy record neuer can be miſt :
That poore retention could not ſo much hold,
Nor need I tallies thy deare loue to skore,
Therefore to giue them from me was I bold,

SHAKE-SPEARES

To truſt thoſe tables that receaue thee more,
To keepe an adiunckt to remember thee,
Were to import forgetfulneſſe in mee.

123

NO! Time, thou ſhalt not boſt that I doe change,
  Thy pyramyds buylt vp with newer might
To me are nothing nouell,nothing ſtrange;
They are but dreſſings of a former ſight:
Our dates are breefe,and therefor we admire,
What thou doſt foyſt vpon vs that is ould,
And rather make them borne to our deſire,
Then thinke that we before haue heard them tould:
Thy regiſters and thee I both defie,
Not wondring at the preſent,nor the paſt,
For thy records,and what we ſee doth lye,
Made more or les by thy continuall haſt:
  This I doe vow and this ſhall euer be,
  I will be true diſpight thy ſyeth and thee.

124

YF my deare loue were but the childe of ſtate,
  It might for fortunes baſterd be vnfathered,
As ſubiect to times loue,or to times hate,
Weeds among weeds,or flowers with flowers gatherd.
No it was buylded far from accident,
It ſuffers not in ſmilinge pomp,nor falls
Vnder the blow of thralled diſcontent,
Whereto th'inuiting time our faſhion calls:
It feares not policy that Heriticke,
Which workes on leaſes of ſhort numbred howers,
But all alone ſtands hugely pollitick,
That it nor growes with heat,nor drownes with ſhowres.
  To this I witnes call the foles of time,
  Which die for goodnes,who haue liu'd for crime.

125

VVEr't ought to me I bore the canopy,
  With my extern the outward honoring,

Or

Here is another warning to WAT, linking again to "time" as
in Sonnet 97.

To truft thofe tables that receaue thee more,
  To keepe an adiunckt to remember thee,
  Were to import forgetfulneffe in mee.

123

NO ! Time, thou fhalt not boft that I doe change.
  Thy pyramyds buylt vp with newer might
To me are nothing nouell, nothing ftrange,
They are but dreffings of a former fight :
Our dates are breefe, and therefor we admire,
What thou doft foyft vpon vs that is ould,
And rather make them borne to our defire,
Then thinke that we before haue heard them tould :
Thy regifters and thee I both defie,
Not wondring at the prefent, nor the paft,
For thy records, and what we fee doth lye,
Made more or les by thy continual haft :
  This I doe vow and this fhall euer be,
  I will be true difpight thy fyeth and thee.

124

YF my deare loue were but the childe of ftate,
  It might for fortunes bafterd be vnfathered,
As fubiect to times loue, or to times hate,
Weeds among weeds, or flowers with flowers gatherd.
No it was buylded far from accident,
It fuffers not in fmilinge pomp, nor falls
Vnder the blow of thralled difcontent,
Whereto th' inuiting time our fafhion calls :
It feares not policy that *Hereticke*,
Which workes on leafes of fhort numbred howers,
But all alone ftands hugely pollitick,
That it nor growes with heat, nor drownes with fhowres.
  To this I witnes call the foles of time,
  Which die for goodnes, who haue liu'd for crime.

125

VVEr't ought to me I bore the canopy,
  With my extern the outward honoring,

Or

SONNETS.

Or layd great bafes for eternity,
Which proues more fhort then waft or ruining?
Haue I not feene dwellers on forme and fauor
Lofe all,and more by paying too much rent
For compound fweet;Forgoing fimple fauor,
Pittifull thriuors in their gazing fpent.
Noe,let me be obfequious in thy heart,
And take thou my oblacion,poore but free,
Which is not mixt with feconds,knows no art,
But mutuall render, onely me for thee.
  Hence,thou fubbornd *Informer*, a trew foule
  When moft impeacht,ftands leaft in thy controule.

VAIN   E

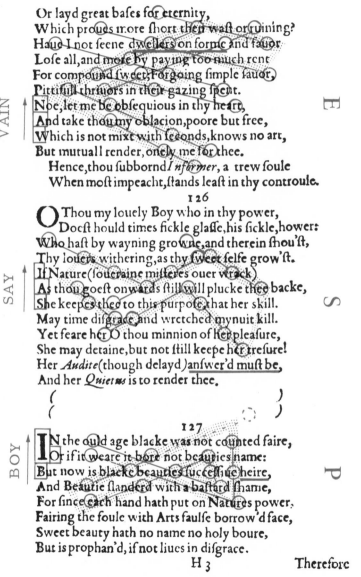

126

O Thou my louely Boy who in thy power,
  Doeft hould times fickle glaffe,his fickle,hower:
Who haft by wayning growne,and therein fhou'ft,
Thy louers withering,as thy fweet felfe grow'ft.
If Nature(foueraine miftreffe ouer wrack)
As thou goeft onwards ftill will plucke thee backe,
She keepes thee to this purpofe,that her skill.
May time difgrace,and wretched mynuit kill.
Yet feare her O thou minnion of her pleafure,
She may detaine,but not ftill keepe her trefure!
  Her *Audite*(though delayd)anfwer'd muft be,
  And her *Quietus* is to render thee.
  (   )
  (   )

SAY   S

127

IN the ould age blacke was not counted faire,
  Or if it weare it bore not beauties name:
But now is blacke beauties fucceffiue heire,
And Beautie flanderd with a baftard fhame,
For fince each hand hath put on Natures power,
Fairing the foule with Arts faulfe borrow'd face,
Sweet beauty hath no name no holy boure,
But is prophan'd, if not liues in difgrace.

BOY   P

H 3   Therefore

It would be interesting to know if the missing two lines of
Sonnet 126 were ever composed at all. Possibly they may have
been too personal or too vulgar for print.

Or layd great bafes for eternity,
Which proues more fhort then waft or ruining ?
Haue I not feene dwellers on forme and fauor
Lofe all, and more by paying too much rent
For compound fweet ; Forgoing fimple fauor,
Pittifull thriuors in their gazing fpent.
Noe, let me be obfequious in thy heart,
And take thou my oblacion, poore but free,
Which is not mixt with feconds, knows no art,
But mutuall render, onely me for thee.
Hence, thou fubbornd *Informer*, a trew foule
When moft impeacht, ftands leaft in thy controule.

126

O Thou my louely Boy who in thy power,
  Doeft hould times fickle glaffe, his fickle, hower :
Who haft by wayning growne, and therein fhou'ft,
Thy louers withering, as thy fweet felfe grow'ft.
If Nature (foueraine mifteres ouer wrack)
As thou goeft onwards ftill will plucke thee backe,
She keepes thee to this purpofe, that her skill.
May time difgrace, and wretched mynuit kill.
Yet feare her O thou minnion of her pleafure,
She may detaine, but not ftill keepe her trefure !
Her *Audite* (though delayd*)* anfwer'd muft be,
And her *Quietus* is to render thee.
  (   )
  (   )

127

IN the ould age blacke was not counted faire,
  Or if it weare it bore not beauties name :
But now is blacke beauties fucceffiue heire,
And Beautie flanderd with a baftard fhame,
For fince each hand hath put on Natures power,
Fairing the foule with Arts faulfe borrow'd face,
Sweet beauty hath no name no holy boure,
But is prophan'd, if not liues in disgrace.

H 3   Therefore

Therefore my Mistersse eyes are Rauen blacke,
Her eyes so sured, and they mourners seeme,
At such who not borne faire no beauty lack,
Slandring Creation with a false esteeme,
　Yet so they mourne becomming of their woe,
　That euery toung saies beauty should looke so.

SIGHT

E

128

HOw oft when thou my musike musike playst,
　Vpon that blessed wood whose motion sounds
With thy sweet fingers when thou gently swayst,
The wiry concord that mine eare confounds,
Do I enuie those Iackes that nimble leape,
To kisse the tender inward of thy hand,
Whilst my poore lips which should that haruest reape,
At the woods bouldnes by thee blushing stand.
To be so tikled they would change their state,
And situation with those dancing chips,
Ore whome their fingers walke with gentle gate,
Making dead wood more blest then liuing lips,
　Since sausie Iackes so happy are in this,
　Giue them their fingers, me thy lips to kisse.

WAIT

A

129

TH'expence of Spirit in a waste of shame
　Is lust in action, and till action, lust
Is periurd, murdrous, blouddy full of blame,
Sauage, extreame, rude, cruell, not to trust,
Inioyd no sooner but dispised straight,
Past reason hunted, and no sooner had
Past reason hated as a swollowed bayt,
On purpose layd to make the taker mad.
Made In pursut and in possession so,
Had, hauing, and in quest, to haue extreame,
A blisse in proofe and proud and very wo,
Before a ioy propofd behind a dreame,
　All this the world well knowes yet none knowes well,
　To shun the heauen that leads men to this hell.

BAIT

R

My

The signal BAT for "Bayt" should be noted for a later oc-
casion when it is used with special significance.

Therefore my Mifterffe eyes are Rauen blacke,
Her eyes fo futed, and they mourners feeme,
At fuch who not borne faire no beauty lack,
Slandring Creation with a falfe efteeme,
 Yet fo they mourne becomming of their woe,
 That euery toung faies beauty fhould looke fo.

128

HOw oft when thou my mufike mufike playft,
 Vpon that bleffed wood whofe motion founds
With thy fweet fingers when thou gently fwayft,
The wiry concord that mine eare confounds,
Do I enuie thofe Iackes that nimble leape,
To kiffe the tender inward of thy hand,
Whilft my poore lips which fhould that harueft reape,
At the woods bouldnes by thee blufhing ftand.
To be fo tikled they would change their ftate,
And fituation with thofe dancing chips,
Ore whome their fingers walke with gentle gate,
Making dead wood more bleft then liuing lips,
 Since faufie Iackes fo happy are in this,
 Giue them their fingers, me thy lips to kiffe.

129

TH' expence of Spirit in a wafte of fhame
 Is luft in action, and till action, luft
Is periurd, murdrous, blouddy full of blame,
Sauage, extreame, rude, cruell, not to truft,
Inioyd no fooner but difpifed ftraight,
Paft reafon, hunted, and no fooner had
Paft reafon hated as a fwollowed bayt,
On purpofe layd to make the taker mad.
Made In purfut and in poffeffion fo,
Had, hauing, and in queft, to haue extreame,
A bliffe in proofe and proud and very wo,
Before a ioy propofd behind a dreame,
 All this the world well knowes yet none knowes well,
 To fhun the heauen that leads men to this hell.
         My

SONNETS.

130

MY Miſtres eyes are nothing like the Sunne,
Currall is farre more red,then her lips red,
If ſnow be white,why then her breſts are dun:
If haires be wiers,black wiers grow on her head:
I haue ſeene Roſes damaskt,red and white,
But no ſuch Roſes ſee I in her cheekes,
And in ſome perfumes is there more delight,
Then in the breath that from my Miſtres reekes.
I loue to heare her ſpeake,yet well I know,
That Muſicke hath a farre more pleaſing ſound:
I graunt I neuer ſaw a goddeſſe goe,
My Miſtres when ſhee walkes treads on the ground.
  And yet by heauen I thinke my loue as rare,
  As any ſhe beli'd with falſe compare.

131

THou art as tiranous,ſo as thou art,
As thoſe whoſe beauties proudly make them cruell;
For well thou know'ſt to my deare doting hart
Thou art the faireſt and moſt precious Iewell.
Yet in good faith ſome ſay that thee behold,
Thy face hath not the power to make loue grone;
To ſay they erre,I dare not be ſo bold,
Although I ſweare it to my ſelfe alone.
And to be ſure that is not falſe I ſweare
A thouſand grones but thinking on thy face,
One on anothers necke do witneſſe beare
Thy blacke is faireſt in my iudgements place.
  In nothing art thou blacke ſaue in thy deeds,
  And thence this ſlaunder as I thinke proceeds.

132

THine eies I loue,and they as pittying me,
Knowing thy heart torment me with diſdaine,
Haue put on black,and louing mourners bee,
Looking with pretty ruth vpon my paine.

And

This E completes the unbelievably difficult series—WILLIAM
SHAKESPEARE—in block letters uniformly oriented.

Here starts another SHAKESPEARE in block letters but this
time the letters are squeezed in at a rate of one per Sonnet.
The signal FAT here links with the thought of double chins
"one on another's necke" as well as telling the reader that the
fat letters continue.

130

MY Miſtres eyes are nothing like the Sunne,
   Currall is farre more red, then her lips red,
If ſnow be white, why then her breſts are dun :
If haires be wiers, black wiers grow on her head :
I haue ſeenes Roſes damaskt, red and white,
But no ſuch Roſes ſee I in her cheekes,
And in ſome perfumes is there more delight,
Then in the breath that from my Miſtres reekes.
I loue to heare her ſpeake, yet well I know,
That Muſicke hath a farre more pleaſing ſound :
I graunt I neuer ſaw a goddeſſe goe,
My Miſtres when ſhee walkes treads on the ground.
  And yet by heauen I thinke my loue as rare,
  As any ſhe beli'd with falſe compare.

131

THou art as tiranous, ſo as thou art,
   As thoſe whoſe beauties proudly make them cruell ;
For well thou know'ſt to my deare doting hart
Thou art the faireſt and moſt precious Iewell.
Yet in good faith ſome ſay that thee behold,
Thy face hath not the power to make loue grone ;
To ſay they erre, I dare not be ſo bold,
Although I ſweare it to my ſelfe alone.
And to be ſure that is not falſe I ſweare
A thouſand grones but thinking on thy face,
One on anothers necke do witneſſe beare
Thy blacke is faireſt in my iudgements place.
  In nothing art thou blacke ſaue in thy deeds,
And thence this ſlaunder as I thinke proceeds.

132

THine eies I loue, and they as pittying me,
   Knowing thy heart torment me with diſdaine,
Haue put on black, and louing mourners bee,
Looking with pretty ruth vpon my paine.
                               And

And truly not the morning Sun of Heauen
Better becomes the gray cheeks of th' East,
Nor that full Starre that vshers in the Eauen
Doth halfe that glory to the sober West
As those two morning eyes become thy face:
O let it then as well beleeme thy heart
To mourne for me since mourning doth thee grace,
And sute thy pitty like in euery part.
    Then will I sweare beauty her selfe is blacke,
    And all they foule that thy complexion lacke.

133

BEshrew that heart that makes my heart to groane
For that deepe wound it giues my friend and me;
I'st not ynough to torture me alone,
But slaue to slauery my sweet'st friend must be.
Me from my selfe thy cruell eye hath taken,
And my next selfe thou harder hast ingrossed,
Of him, my selfe, and thee I am forsaken,
A torment thrice three-fold thus to be crossed:
Prison my heart in thy steele bosomes warde,
But then my friends heart let my poore heart bale,
Who ere keepes me, let my heart be his garde,
Thou canst not then vse rigor in my Iaile.
    And yet thou wilt, for I being pent in thee,
    Perforce am thine and all that is in me.

134

SO now I haue confest that he is thine,
And I my selfe am morgag'd to thy will,
My selfe Ile forfeit, so that other mine,
Thou wilt restore to be my comfort still:
But thou wilt not, nor he will not be free,
For thou art couetous, and he is kinde,
He learnd but suretie-like to write for me,
Vnder that bond that him as fast doth binde.
The statute of thy beauty thou wilt take,
Thou vsurer that put'st forth all to vse,

And

The association of "foule" and TOAD with the preceding fat double chin idea suggests that the author meant to express his contempt for the person to whom Sonnets 130 to 134 were addressed. It could have been the queen, who is known to have loved the vain flattery of her courtiers long after her beauty had turned to ugliness. The general tone of these four sonnets is thinly veiled disgust coupled with an enduring love, nevertheless.

And truly not the morning Sun of Heauen
Better becomes the gray cheeks of th' Eaſt
Nor that full Starre that vſhers in the Eauen
Doth halfe that glory to the ſober Weſt
As thoſe two morning eyes become thy face :
O let it then as well beſeeme thy heart
To mourne for me ſince mourning doth thee grace,
And ſute thy pitty like in euery part.
   Then will I ſweare beauty her ſelfe is blacke,
   And all they foule that thy complexion lacke.

133

BEſhrew that heart that makes my heart to groane
  For that deepe wound it giues my friend and me ;
I'ſt not ynough to torture me alone,
But ſlaue to ſlauery my ſweet'ſt friend muſt be.
Me from my ſelfe thy cruell eye hath taken,
And my next ſelfe thou harder haſt ingroſſed,
Of him, my ſelfe, and thee I am forſaken,
A torment thrice three-fold thus to be croſſed :
Priſon my heart in thy ſteele boſomes warde,
But then my friends heart let my poore heart bale,
Who ere keepes me, let my heart be his garde,
Thou canſt not then vſe rigor in my Iaile.
   And yet thou wilt, for I being pent in thee,
   Perforce am thine and all that is in me.

134

SO now I haue confeſt that he is thine,
  And I my ſelfe am morgag'd to thy will,
My ſelfe Ile forfeit, ſo that other mine,
Thou wilt reſtore to be my comfort ſtill :
But thou wilt not, nor he will not be free,
For thou art couetous, and he is kinde,
He learnd but ſuritie-like to write for me,
Vnder that bond that him as faſt doth binde.
The ſtatute of thy beauty thou wilt take,
Thou vſurer that put'ſt forth all to vſe,

And

140

And fue a friend, came debter for my fake,
So him I loofe through my vnkinde abufe.
  Him haue I loft, thou haft both him and me,
  He paies the whole, and yet am I not free.

135

WHo euer hath her wifh, thou haft thy *Will*,
    And *Will* too boote, and *Will* in ouer-plus,
More then enough am I that vexe thee ftill,
To thy fweet will making addition thus.
Wilt thou whofe will is large and fpatious,
Not once vouchfafe to hide my will in thine,
Shall will in others feeme right gracious,
And in my will no faire acceptance fhine:
The fea all water, yet receiues raine ftill,
And in aboundance addeth to his ftore,
So thou beeing rich in *Will* adde to thy *Will*,
One will of mine to make thy large *Will* more.
  Let no vnkinde, no faire befeechers kill,
  Thinke all but one, and me in that one *Will*.

136

IF thy foule check thee that I come fo neere,
  Sweare to thy blind foule that I was thy *Will*,
And will thy foule knowes is admitted there,
Thus farre for loue, my loue-fute fweet fullfill.
Will, will fulfill the treafure of thy loue,
I fill it full with wils, and my will one,
In things of great receit with eafe we proue,
Among a number one is reckon'd none.
Then in the number let me paffe vntold,
Though in thy ftores account I one muft be,
For nothing hold me, fo it pleafe thee hold,
That nothing me, a fome-thing fweet to thee.
  Make but my name thy loue, and loue that ftill,
  And then thou loueft me for my name is *Will*.

137

THou blinde foole loue, what dooft thou to mine eyes,
              I   That

E

S

SATE

SATE

Here is a fine example of the confirmation of a doubtful point
by immediate repetition. Any question about reading SAT
as "Sate" to link with "over-plus" disappears when the same
signal shows up in the next Sonnet and there links with "fill
it full." This gambit has been used many times in the plays.

And fue a friend, came debter for my fake,
So him I loofe through my vnkinde abufe.
   Him haue I loft, thou haft both him and me,
   He paies the whole, and yet am I not free.

135

WHo euer hath her wifh, thou haft thy *Will*,
   And *Will* too boote, and *Will* in ouer-plus,
More then enough am I that vexe thee ftill,
To thy fweet will making addition thus.
Wilt thou whofe will is large and fpatious,
Not once vouchfafe to hide my will in thine,
Shall will in others feeme right gracious,
And in my will no faire acceptance fhine :
The fea all water, yet receiues raine ftill,
And in aboundance addeth to his ftore,
So thou beeing rich in *Will* adde to thy *Will*,
One will of mine to make thy large *Will* more.
   Let no vnkinde, no faire befeechers kill,
   Thinke all but one, and me in that one *Will*.

136

IF thy foule check thee that I come fo neere,
   Sweare to thy blind foule that I was thy *Will*,
And will thy foule knowes is admitted there,
Thus farre for loue, my loue-fute fweet fullfill.
Will, will fullfill the treafure of thy loue,
I fill it full with wils, and my will one,
In things of great receit with eafe we prooue.
Among a number one is reckon'd none.
Then in the number let me paffe vntold,
Though in thy ftores account I one muft be,
For nothing hold me, fo it pleafe thee hold,
That nothing me, a fome-thing fweet to thee.
   Make but my name thy loue, and loue that ftill,
   And then thou loueft me for my name is *Will*.

137

THou blinde foole loue, what dooft thou to mine eyes,
                I   That

That they behold and fee not what they fee :
They know what beautie is, fee where it lyes,
Yet what the beft is, take the worft to be.
If eyes corrupt by ouer-partiall lookes,
Be anchord in the baye where all men ride,
Why of eyes falfehood haft thou forged hookes,
Whereto the iudgement of my heart is tide?
Why fhould my heart thinke that a feuerall plot,
Which my heart knowes the wide worlds common place?
Or mine eyes feeing this,fay this is not
To put faire truth vpon fo foule a face,
  In things right true my heart and eyes haue erred,
  And to this falfe plague are they now transferred.

P

138

*W*Hen my loue fweares that fhe is made of truth,
  I do beleeue her though I know fhe lyes,
That fhe might thinke me fome vntuterd youth,
Vnlearned in the worlds falfe fubtilties.
Thus vainely thinking that fhe thinkes me young,
Although fhe knowes my dayes are paft the beft,
Simply I credit her falfe fpeaking tongue,
On both fides thus is fimple truth fuppreft :
But wherefore fayes fhe not fhe is vniuft ?
And wherefore fay not I that I am old ?
O loues beft habit is in feeming truft,
And age in loue,loues not t'haue yeares told.
  Therefore I lye with her,and fhe with me,
  And in our faults by lyes we flattered be,

E

139

O Call not me to iuftifie the wrong,
  That thy vnkindneffe layes vpon my heart,
Wound me not with thine eye but with th' toung,
Vfe power with power,and flay me not by Art,
Tell me thou lou'ft elfe-where;but in my fight,
Deare heart forbeare to glance thine eye afide,
What needft thou wound with cunning when thy might

Is

Perhaps the reappearance of WIT here implies that the reader must use an extra dose of it if he is to find the awkwardly placed namesticks which form this block E.

That they behold and fee not what they fee:
They know what beautie is, fee where it lyes,
Yet what the beſt is, take the worſt to be.
If eyes corrupt by ouer-partiall lookes,
Be anchord in the baye where all men ride,
Why of eyes falſehood haſt thou forged hookes,
Whereto the iudgement of my heart is tide?
Why ſhould my heart thinke that a feuerall plot,
Which my heart knowes the wide worlds common place?
Or mine eyes feeing this, ſay this is not
To put faire truth vpon ſo foule a face,
    In things right true my heart and eyes haue erred,
    And to this falſe plague are they now tranſferred.

138

W Hen my loue ſweares that ſhe is made of truth,
    I do beleeue her though I know ſhe lyes,
That ſhe might thinke me ſome vntuterd youth,
Vnlearned in the worlds falſe ſubtilties.
Thus vainely thinking that ſhe thinkes me young,
Although ſhe knowes my dayes are paſt the beſt,
Simply I credit her falſe ſpeaking tongue,
On both ſides thus is ſimple truth ſuppreſt:
But wherefore ſayes ſhe not ſhe is vniuſt?
And wherefore ſay not I that I am old?
O loues beſt habit is in feeming truſt,
And age in loue, loues not t'haue yeares told.
    Therefore I lye with her, and ſhe with me,
    And in our faults by lyes we flattered be.

139

O Call not me to iuſtifie the wrong,
    That thy vnkindneſſe layes vpon my heart,
Wound me not with thine eye but with thy toung,
Vſe power with power, and ſlay me not by Art,
Tell me thou lou'ſt elſe-where ; but in my fight,
Deare heart forbeare to glance thine eye aſide,
What needſt thou wound with cunning when thy might
                                                    Is

SONNETS.

Is more then my ore-preſt defence can bide?
Let me excuſe thee,ah my loue well knowes,
Her prettie lookes haue beene mine enemies,
And therefore from my face ſhe turnes my foes,
That they elſe-where might dart their iniuries :
　Yet do not ſo,but ſince I am neere ſlaine,
　Kill me out-right with lookes,and rid my paine.

HATE

140

BE wiſe as thou art cruell,do not preſſe
My toung-tide patience with too much diſdaine :
Leaſt ſorrow lend me words and words expreſſe,
The manner of my pittie wanting paine.
If I might teach thee witte better it weare,
Though not to loue,yet loue to tell me ſo,
As teſtie ſick-men when their deaths be neere,
No newes but health from their Phiſitions know.
For if I ſhould diſpaire I ſhould grow madde,
And in my madneſſe might ſpeake ill of thee,
Now this ill wreſting world is growne ſo bad,
Madde ſlanderers by madde eares beleeued be.
　That I may not be ſo, nor thou be lyde,　(wide.
　Beare thine eyes ſtraight , though thy proud heart goe

TA'EN

A

R

141

IN faith I doe not loue thee with mine eyes,
For they in thee a thouſand errors note,
But tis my heart that loues what they diſpiſe,
Who in diſpight of view is pleaſd to dote.
Nor are mine eares with thy toungs tune delighted,
Nor tender feeling to baſe touches prone,
Nor taſte, nor ſmell, deſire to be inuited
To any ſenſuall feaſt with thee alone :
But my fiue wits,nor my fiue ſences can
Diſwade one fooliſh heart from ſeruing thee,
Who leaues vnſwai'd the likeneſſe of a man,
Thy proud hearts ſlaue and vaſſall wretch to be :
　Onely my plague thus farre I count my gaine,
　That ſhe that makes me ſinne,awards me paine.

E

TOTE

I 2　　　Loue

"Taken in death" is the linking thought for Sonnet 140.
Notice that the block A over-flows well into the next Sonnet
but this is compensated by squeezing the R into the same
Sonnet.

Is more then my ore-preſt defence can bide?
Let me excuſe thee, ah my loue well knowes,
Her prettie lookes haue beene mine enemies,
And therefore from my face ſhe turnes my foes,
That they elſe-where might dart their iniuries :
    Yet do not ſo, but ſince I am neere ſlaine,
    Kill me out-right with lookes, and rid my paine.

140

BE wiſe as thou art cruell, do not preſſe
  My toung-tide patience with too much diſdaine :
Leaſt ſorrow lend me words and words expreſſe,
The manner of my pittie wanting paine.
If I might teach thee witte better it weare,
Though not to loue, yet loue to tell me ſo,
As teſtie ſick-men when their deaths be neere,
No newes but health from their Phiſitions know.
For if I ſhould diſpaire I ſhould grow madde,
And in my madneſſe might ſpeake ill of thee,
Now this ill wreſting world is growne ſo bad,
Madde ſlanderers by madde eares beleeued be.
    That I may not be ſo, nor thou be lyde,   (wide.
    Beare thine eyes ſtraight, though thy proud heart goe

141

IN faith I doe not loue thee with mine eyes,
  For they in thee a thouſand errors note,
But 'tis my heart that loues what they diſpiſe,
Who in diſpight of view is pleaſd to dote.
Nor are mine eares with thy toungs tune delighted,
Nor tender feeling to baſe touches prone,
Nor taſte, nor ſmell, deſire to be inuited
To any ſenſuall feaſt with thee alone :
But my fiue wits, nor my fiue ſences can
Diſwade one fooliſh heart from ſeruing thee,
Who leaues vnſwal'd the likeneſſe of a man,
Thy proud hearts ſlaue and vaſſall wretch to be :
    Onely my plague thus farre I count my gaine,
    That ſhe that makes me ſinne, awards me paine.
                I 2   Loue

142

LOue is my finne, and thy deare vertue hate,
Hate of my finne, grounded on finfull louing,
O but with mine, compare thou thine owne ftate,
And thou fhalt finde it merrits not reproouing,
Or if it do, not from thofe lips of thine,
That haue prophan'd their fcarlet ornaments,
And feald falfe bonds of loue as oft as mine,
Robd others beds reuenues of their rents.
Be it lawfull I loue thee as thou lou'ft thofe,
Whome thine eyes wooe as mine importune thee,
Roote pittie in thy heart that when it growes,
Thy pitty may deferue to pittied bee.
    If thou dooft feeke to haue what thou dooft hide,
    By felfe example mai'ft thou be denide.

143

LOe as a carefull hufwife runnes to catch,
One of her fethered creatures broake away,
Sets downe her babe and makes all fwift difpatch
In purfuit of the thing fhe would haue ftay:
Whilft her neglected child holds her in chafe,
Cries to catch her whofe bufie care is bent,
To follow that which flies before her face:
Not prizing her poore infants difcontent;
So runft thou after that which flies from thee,
Whilft I thy babe chace thee a farre behind,
But if thou catch thy hope turne back to me:
And play the mothers part kifle me, be kind.
    So will I pray that thou maift haue thy *Will*,
    If thou turne back and my loude crying ftill.

144

TWo loues I haue of comfort and difpaire,
Which like two fpirits do fugieft me ftill,
The better angell is a man right faire:
The worfer fpirit a woman collour'd il.
To win me foone to hell my femall euill,

Tempteth

This is the start of the final "SHAKESPEARE." Here the author will attempt to place each block letter entirely within a single Sonnet and keep up the pace of one letter per Sonnet.

142

LOue is my finne, and thy deare vertue hate,
   Hate of my finne, grounded on finfull louing,
O but with mine, compare thou thine owne ftate,
And thou fhalt finde it merrits not reproouing,
Or if it do, not from thofe lips of thine,
That haue prophan'd their fcarlet ornaments,
And feald falfe bonds of loue as oft as mine,
Robd others beds reuenues of their rents.
Be it lawfull I loue thee as thou lou'ft thofe,
Whome thine eyes wooe as mine importune thee,
Roote pittie in thy heart that when it growes,
Thy pitty may deferue to pittied bee.
   If thou dooft feeke to haue what thou dooft hide,
   By felfe example mai'ft thou be denide.

143

LOe as a carefull hufwife runnes to catch,
   One of her fethered creatures broake away,
Sets downe her babe and makes all fwift difpatch
In purfuit of the thing fhe would haue ftay :
Whilft her neglected child holds her in chace,
Cries to catch her whofe bufie care is bent,
To follow that which flies before her face :
Not prizing her poore infants difcontent ;
So runft thou after that which flies from thee,
Whilft I thy babe chace thee a farre behind,
But if thou catch thy hope turne back to me:
And play the mothers part kiffe me, be kind.
   So will I pray that thou maift haue thy *Will*,
   If thou turne back and my loude crying ftill.

144

TWo loues I haue of comfort and difpaire,
   Which like two fpirits do fugieft me ftill,
The better angell is a man right faire :
The worfer fpirit a woman collour'd il.
To win me foone to hell my femall euill,

                                        Tempteth

148

WAIT

Tempteth my better angel from my fight,
And would corrupt my faint to be a diuel:
Wooing his purity with her fowle pride.
And whether that my angel be turn'd finde,
Suspect I may, yet not directly tell,
But being both from me both to each friend,
I gesse one angel in an others hel.
　Yet this fhal I nere know but liue in doubt,
　Till my bad angel fire my good one out.

A

145

THofe lips that Loues owne hand did make,
　Breath'd forth the found that faid I hate,
To me that languifht for her fake:
But when fhe faw my wofull ftate,
Straight in her heart did mercie come,
Chiding that tongue that euer fweet,
Was vfde in giuing gentle dome;
And tought it thus a new to greete:
I hate fhe alterd with an end,
That follow'd it as gentle day,
Doth follow night who like a fiend
From heauen to hell is flowne away.
　I hate, from hate away fhe threw,
　And fau'd my life faying not you.

?

146

POore foule the center of my finfull earth,
　My finfull earth thefe rebbell powres that thee array,
Why doft thou pine within and fuffer dearth
Painting thy outward walls fo coftlie gay?
Why fo large coft hauing fo fhort a leafe,
Doft thou vpon thy fading manfion fpend?
Shall wormes inheritors of this exceffe,
Eate vp thy charge? is this thy bodies end?
Then foule liue thou vpon thy feruants loffe,
And let that pine to aggrauat thy ftore;
Buy tearmes diuine in felling houres of droffe:

BAIT

?

13　　　　　　　　　　　　Within

The game at this point is both a trial and a triumph. It is un-
thinkable to stop after a continuous series of about a hundred
large letters without a break. Yet here is a definite hiatus after
SHA. Hours of search fail to reveal a significant large letter
pattern in Sonnets 145 and 146. Does this mean the end? But
no, the marginal signals tell the reader to WAT and again to
WAIT. This hiatus is just BATE to tease the reader hastening
to complete this last SHAKESPEARE. See Sonnet 5.

Tempteth my better angel from my fight,
And would corrupt my faint to be a diuel :
Wooing his purity with her fowle pride.
And whether that my angel be turn'd finde,
Sufpect I may, yet not directly tell,
But being both from me both to each friend,
I geffe one angel in an others hel.
 Yet this fhal I nere know but liue in doubt,
 Till my bad angel fire my good one out.

145

THofe lips that Loues owne hand did make,
 Breath'd forth the found that faid I hate,
To me that languifht for her fake :
But when fhe faw my wofull ftate,
Straight in her heart did mercie come,
Chiding that tongue that euer fweet,
Was vfde in giuing gentle dome :
And tought it thus a new to greete :
I hate fhe alterd with an end,
That follow'd it as gentle day,
Doth follow night who like a fiend
From heauen to hell is flowne away.
 I hate, from hate away fhe threw,
 And fau'd my life faying not you.

146

POore foule the center of my finfull earth,
 My finfull earth thefe rebbell powres that thee array,
Why doft thou pine within and fuffer dearth
Painting thy outward walls fo coftlie gay ?
Why fo large coft hauing fo fhort a leafe,
Doft thou vpon thy fading manfion fpend ?
Shall wormes inheritors of this exceffe
Eate vp thy charge ? is this thy bodies end ?
Then foule liue thou vpon thy feruants loffe,
And let that pine to aggrauat thy ftore ;
Buy tearmes diuine in felling houres of droffe :

Within

Within be fed, without be rich no more,
    So shalt thou feed on death,that feeds on men,
    And death once dead,ther's.no more dying then,

147

MY loue is as a feauer longing still,
    For that which longer nurseth the disease,
Feeding on that which doth preserue the ill,
Th'vncertaine sicklie appetite to please:
My reason the Phisition to my loue,
Angry that his prescriptions are not kept,
Hath left me,and I desperate now approoue,
Desire is death,which Phisick did except.
Past cure I am,now Reason is past care,
And frantick madde with euer-more vnrest,
My thoughts and my discourse as mad mens are,
At randon from the truth vainely exprest.
    For I haue sworne thee faire,and thought thee bright,
    Who art as black as hell,as darke as night.

148

O Me ! what eyes hath loue put in my head,
    Which haue no correspondence with true sight,
Or if they haue,where is my iudgment fled,
That censures falsely what they see aright ?
If that be faire whereon my false eyes dote,
What meanes the world to say it is not so ?
If it be not,then loue doth well denote,
Loues eye is not so true as all mens:no,
How can it ? O how can loues eye be true,
That is so vext with watching and with teares?
No maruaile then though I mistake my view,
The sunne it selfe sees not,till heauen cleeres.
    O cunning loue,with teares thou keepst me blinde,
    Least eyes well seeing thy foule faults should finde,

149

CAnst thou O cruell,say I loue thee not,
    When I against my selfe with thee pertake :

Doe

MA(H)D

K

E

Now the letters continue in easily discovered patterns and the
author chides us with MA(H)D WIT in the margin.

Within be fed, without be rich no more,
  So fhalt thou feed on death, that feeds on men.
  And death once dead, ther's no more dying then.

147

MY loue is as a feauer longing ftill,
  For that which longer nurfeth the difeafe,
Feeding on that which doth preferue the ill,
Th' vncertaine ficklie appetite to pleafe:
My reafon the Phifition to my loue,
Angry that his prefcriptions are not kept
Hath left me, and I defperate now approoue,
Defire is death, which Phifick did except.
Paft cure I am, now Reafon is paft care,
And frantick madde with euer-more vnreft,
My thoughts and my difcourfe as mad mens are,
At randon from the truth vainely expreft.
  For I haue fworne thee faire, and thought thee bright,
  Who art as black as hell, as darke as night.

148

O Me! what eyes hath loue put in my head,
  Which haue no correfpondence with true fight,
Or if they haue, where is my iudgment fled,
That cenfures falfely what they fee aright?
If that be faire whereon my falfe eyes dote,
What meanes the world to fay it is not fo?
If it be not, then loue doth well denote,
Loues eye is not fo true as all mens: no,
How can it? O how can loues eyes be true,
That is fo vext with watching and with teares?
No maruaile then though I miftake my view,
The funne it felfe fees not, till heauen cleeres.
  O cunning loue, with teares thou keepft me blinde,
  Leaft eyes well feeing thy foule faults fhould finde.

149

CAnft thou O cruell, fay I loue thee not,
  When I againft my felfe with thee pertake:

Doe

152

SONNETS.

Doe I not thinke on thee when I forgot
Am of my felfe, all tirant for thy fake?
Who hateth thee that I doe call my friend,
On whom froun'ft thou that I doe faune vpon,
Nay if thou lowr'ft on me doe I not fpend
Reuenge vpon my felfe with prefent mone?
What merrit do I in my felfe refpect,
That is fo proude thy feruice to difpife,
When all my beft doth worfhip thy defect,
Commanded by the motion of thine eyes.
But loue hate on for now I know thy minde,
Thofe that can fee thou lou'ft,and I am blind.

150

OH from what powre haft thou this powrefull might,
VVith infufficiency my heart to fway,
To make me giue the lie to my true fight,
And fwere that brightneffe doth not grace the day?
Whence haft thou this becomming of things il,
That in the very refule of thy deeds,
There is fuch ftrength and warrantife of skill,
That in my minde thy worft all beft exceeds?
Who taught thee how to make me loue thee more,
The more I heare and fee iuft caufe of hate,
Oh though I loue what others doe abhor,
VVith others thou fhouldft not abhor my ftate.
If thy vnworthineffe raifd loue in me,
More worthy I to be belou'd of thee.

151

LOue is too young to know what confcience is,
Yet who knowes not confcience is borne of loue,
Then gentle cheater vrge not my amiffe,
Leaft guilty of my faults thy fweet felfe proue.
For thou betraying me, I doe betray
My nobler part to my grofe bodies treafon,
My foule doth tell my body that he may,
Triumph in loue,flefh ftaies no farther reafon,

But

The by now familiar pattern includes another WAT signal
probably acknowledging the poorly formed P and E.

Doe I not thinke on thee when I forgot
Am of my felfe, all tirant for thy fake?
Who hateth thee that I doe call my friend,
On whom froun'ft thou that I doe faune vpon,
Nay if thou lowrft on me doe I not fpend
Reuenge vpon my felfe with prefent mone?
What merrit do I in my felfe refpect,
That is fo proude thy feruice to difpife,
When all my beft doth worfhip thy defect,
Commanded by the motion of thine eyes.
    But loue hate on for now I know thy minde,
    Thofe that can fee thou lou'ft, and I am blind.

150

OH from what powre haft thou this powrefull might,
    VVith infufficiency my heart to fway,
To make me giue the lie to my true fight,
And fwere that brightneffe doth not grace the day?
Whence haft thou this becomming of things il,
That in the very refufe of thy deeds,
There is fuch ftrength and warrantife of skill,
That in my minde thy worft all beft exceeds?
Who taught thee how to make me loue thee more,
The more I heare and fee iuft caufe of hate,
Oh though I loue what others doe abhor,
VVith others thou fhouldft not abhor my ftate.
    If thy vnworthineffe raifd loue in me,
    More worthy I to be belou'd of thee.

151

LOue is too young to know what confcience is,
    Yet who knowes not confcience is borne of loue,
Then gentle cheater vrge not my amiffe,
Leaft guilty of my faults thy fweet felfe proue.
For thou betraying me, I doe betray
My nobler part to my grofe bodies treafon,
My foule doth tell my body that he may,
Triumph in loue, flefh ftaies no farther reafon.
                                        But

But ryfing at thy name doth point out thee,
As his triumphant prize,proud of this pride,
He is contented thy poore drudge to be
To ftand in thy affaires,fall by thy fide.
   No want of confcience hold it that I call,
   Her loue,for whofe deare loue I rife and fall.

152

IN louing thee thou know'ft I am forfworne,
  But thou art twice forfworne to me loue fwearing,
In act thy bed-vow broake and new faith torne,
In vowing new hate after new loue bearing:
But why of two othes breach doe I accufe thee,
When I breake twenty:I am periur'd moft,
For all my vowes are othes but to mifufe thee:
And all my honeft faith in thee is loft.
For I haue fworne deepe othes of thy deepe kindneffe:
Othes of thy loue,thy truth,thy conftancie,
And to inlighten thee gaue eyes to blindneffe,
Or made them fwere againft the thing they fee.
   For I haue fworne thee faire:more periurde eye,
   To fwere againft the truth fo foule a lie.

153

CVpid laid by his brand and fell a fleepe,
  A maide of *Dyans* this aduantage found,
And his loue-kindling fire did quickly fteepe
In a could vallie-fountaine of that ground:
Which borrow'd from this holie fire of loue,
A datelefle liuely heat ftill to indure,
And grew a feething bath which yet men proue,
Againft ftrang malladies a foueraigne cure:
But at my miftres eie loues brand new fired,
The boy for triall needes would touch my breft,
I fick withall the helpe of bath defired,
And thether hied a fad diftemperd gueft.
   But found no cure,the bath for my helpe lies,
   Where *Cupid* got new fire;my miftres eye.

These block letters suffer from substantial deviations from
parallelism and uniformity of spacing of the namesticks. It
is getting near the end and the high beginning standards have
shifted again.

But ryfing at thy name doth point out thee,
As his triumphant prize, proud of this pride,
He is contented thy poore drudge to be
To ftand in thy affaires, fall by thy fide.
   No want of confcience hold it that I call,
   Her loue, for whofe deare loue I rife and fall.

152

IN louing thee thou know'ft I am forfworne,
  But thou art twice forfworne to me loue fwearing ;
In act thy bed-vow broake and new faith torne,
In vowing new hate after new loue bearing :
But why of two othes breach doe I accufe thee,
When I breake twenty : I am periur'd moft,
For all my vowes are othes but to mifufe thee :
And all my honeft faith in thee is loft.
For I haue fworne deepe othes of thy deepe kindneffe :
Othes of thy loue, thy truth, thy conftancie,
And to inlighten thee gaue eyes to blindneffe,
Or made them fwere againft the thing they fee.
   For I haue fworne thee faire : more periurde eye,
   To fwere againft the truth fo foule a lie.

153

CVpid laid by his brand and fell a fleepe,
  A maide of Dyans this aduantage found,
And his loue-kindling fire did quickly fteepe
In a could vallie-fountaine of that ground :
Which borrowd from this holie fire of loue,
A dateleffe liuely heat ftill to indure,
And grew a feething bath which yet men proue,
Againft ftrang malladies a foueraigne cure :
But at my miftres eie loues brand new fired,
The boy for triall needes would touch my breft,
I fick withall the helpe of bath defired,
And thether hied a fad diftemperd gueft.
   But found no cure, the bath for my helpe lies,
   Where Cupid got new fire ; my miftres eye.

156

SONNETS.

154

THe little Loue-God lying once a fleepe,
　Laid by his fide his heart inflaming brand,
Whilſt many Nymphes that vou d chaſt life to keep,
Came tripping by, but in her maiden hand,
The fayreſt votary tooke vp that fire,
Which many Legions of true hearts had warm'd,
And ſo the Generall of hot deſire,
Was ſleeping by a Virgin hand diſarm'd.
This brand ſhe quenched in a coole Well by,
Which from loues fire tooke heat perpetuall,
Growing a bath and healthfull remedy,
For men diſeaſd, but I my Miſtriſſe thrall,
　Came there for cure and this by that I proue,
　Loues fire heates water, water cooles not loue.

AUGHT

E

FINIS.

K A

At last the end, and the modest acknowledgment "Aught"—
"little," something of an understatement.

154

THe little Loue-God lying once a fleepe,
  Laid by his fide his heart inflaming brand,
Whilſt many Nymphes that vou'd chaſt life to keep,
Came tripping by, but in her maiden hand,
The fayreſt votary tooke vp that fire,
Which many Legions of true hearts had warm'd,
And fo the Generall of hot defire,
Was fleeping by a Virgin hand difarm'd.
This brand ſhe quenched in a coole Well by,
Which from loues fire tooke heat perpetuall,
Growing a bath and healthfull remedy,
For men difeafd, but I my Miſtriſſe thrall,
  Came there for cure and this by that I proue,
  Loues fire heates water, water coules not loue.

FINIS.

K   A

CHAPTER 4

ACCIDENT OR INTENT

The natural resistance that most people have to any disturbance of the orthodox view of things leads almost immediately to the query—what is it that is wrong with these Vere acrostics? No literary genius like Shakespeare could possibly descend from the clouds of poetic fancy to bother with such mundane petty details as these. Where is the gimmick? The most obvious answer is simply this: certainly the acrostics are there all right but the same thing could be found anywhere if a sufficient search were made. After all the letter *e* is the most commonly used of the entire alphabet, the letter *r* is quite common and although *v* is not common, the use of the alternates *u* and *w* gives a wide lattitude for finding acrostic Vere's in any English text. This set of acrostics is interesting enough but it is still just the result of pure accident.

Such a view fails to penetrate the surface of the matter. Considering the points one by one, there is first the question as to the "Shakespeare" genius. No ordinary mortal should have the temerity to either expand or contract the limits of ability of any true genius. No one but another genius is qualified to circumscribe his art conjecturally. The orthodox supporters of the Stratford man have not hesitated to ascribe to his "genius" the remarkable disparity between his meagre education and the intimate knowledge which the works demonstrate of such things as law, hawking, the English and foreign courts and travel in Italy. Where the works clearly show a knowledge impossible to have been acquired in Stratford it has been readily explained as evidence of the exceptional genius he possessed. Why shouldn't the creation of these intricate acrostic patterns be also within the ambit of talent of this outstanding author? Of course they should—and the only difficulty is that they show the author to be someone else.

Secondly, there is the question of taking enough time to find the same thing elsewhere. How long would it require? It required only two months of spare time outside of a regular full-time employment for the present author to locate the 1,000 odd acrostics—with their signals and links—in the 154 Sonnets. How long it would take to find the same thing elsewhere can only be conjectured.

Thirdly, it can be asserted that the Vere acrostics themselves exist everywhere. So they do—here is an example from the "breeches" Bible printed in London in 1605. The twenty-third psalm here contains four acrostic Vere's. And surely Edward de Vere didn't write or translate *this*.

160

PSAL. XXIII.

1 *Becaufe the Prophet had prooued the great mercies of God at diuers times, and in fundry maners, he gathereth a certaine affurance, fully perfwading himfelfe that God wil continue the very fame goodneffe toward him for euer.*

❡ A Pſalme of Dauid.

THe Lord is my * ſhepheard, * I ſhall not want.

2 He maketh me to reſt in greene paſture, and leadeth me by the ſtill waters.

3 He reſtoreth my ſoule, and leadeth me in the ᶜ paths of righteouſnes for his Names ſake.

4 Yea, though I ſhould walke through the valley of the ᵈ ſhadow of death, I will feare no euill: for thou ❛ with me, thy rod and thy ſtaffe, they comfort me.

5 Thou doeſt prepare a ❛ table before me in the ſight of mine aduerſaries: thou doeſt ᶠ anoynt mine head with oyle, and my cup runneth ouer.

6 Doubtleſſe, kindnes & mercy ſhall follow me all the dayes of my life, & I ſhall remain a long ſeaſon in the ᵍ houſe of the Lord.

But this begs the question. It is not how frequently do acrostic Vere's appear in a typical English text but rather what is the probability that such acrostics will occur in the patterns or arrangements which appear in these Sonnets. It is easy to find one Vere almost anywhere. It is not so easy, but yet possible, to find a second one crossing it to form a letter X. It is really difficult to find four of them arranged in a square pattern to form an O or a D. It is practically impossible to find dozens of them arranged to form letters which fall in proper sequence to spell a word, a name, or a series of them. This can be demonstrated mathematically by the principles of probability. (Non-mathematicians can find the principles simply explained in the *Encyclopaedia Brittanica*.)

What can the laws of probability do to show whether the acrostic patterns (not the acrostics individually) are accidental or intentional? Is this question capable of mathematical treatment? The following demonstration will show that the mathematics of probability can be applied to the problem in a way that is easily understood by the layman without getting beyond simple fractions and the multiplication table.

Consider for a test sample the acrostic patterns found in Sonnets 37 through 42. Here there are twenty-one acrostic Vere's which are arranged to form the six letters $\diamondsuit \times \vdash \diamondsuit \, \mathsf{R} \, \square$. These six Sonnets each contain fourteen lines, and the average line length is 43 characters and spaces. 6 x 14 x 43 = 3612, the total number of spaces in which could be found either an *e*, an *r*, a *v*, a *u*, or a *w* if the letters had fallen on the page entirely by accident. But these pages were composed intentionally as inspired poetry and the question is whether they were composed so as to also intentionally contain 21 acrostic Vere's spelling Oxford. Consider then some other piece of text the same size. It can be any text so long as it has 84 lines of 43 spaces average length. It is bound to contain a lot of v's, e's, r's, u's, and w's; just how many on the average can be determined by consulting the recognized frequency tables. But that won't be necessary for right at the start there are two concessions which can be made, both of them in favor of accident rather than intent.

Let it be conceded first that *every* page of English text 84 lines long and 43 characters wide will, by accident, contain 21 acrostic Vere's arranged in some random pattern. Let it also be conceded that six of them will be so located that they will form in sequence one leg of each of the six letters of Oxford. These assumptions are perfectly valid because to contradict them would be to admit at the start that the acrostically formed large letters could not exist by accident and therefore must have been intentionally introduced. It now remains to be determined just what the probability is that the remaining fifteen of them will be so located that they will complete these six letters. For if just one of the fifteen is out of place the pattern will not spell OXFORD. That probability can be determined as follows:

1. Locate the Vere that is suitable for a starting leg of the first O in Oxford and which it is conceded every text will be bound to have by accident. For example:

e

r

e

v

2. In order to be useful the next Vere must be positioned in a suitable relation to the first one so that it can become the second leg of the O.

3. It must have one end near the an end of the first Vere. A tolerance of three spaces vertically and ten spaces horizontally can be allowed which gives an area of thirty spaces out of the 3612 in which a second Vere must begin (or end).

e

r

□□□□□□□□□ e
□□□□□□ v □□□
□□□□□□□□□□

4. It must also lie in a suitable direction. If there is a total of nine possible directions in which any Vere can lie, then no more than three of them can be useful.

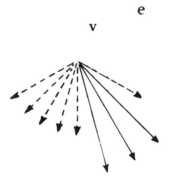

5. The chance that one of the fifteen remaining Vere's will have its end and its direction suitable is $\dfrac{30}{3612} \times \dfrac{3}{9} = \dfrac{90}{32508}$ which is $\dfrac{1}{361}$

6. If the 1 chance out of 361 did occur there would be a second Vere located within the tolerances specified. Thus there will be found the two legs of the first letter O in one out of every 361 pieces of text, on the average.

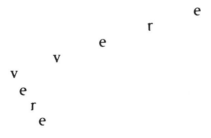

7. With these in place the chance of finding a third Vere suitably positioned to form the third leg of the O is again about 1 in 361.

164

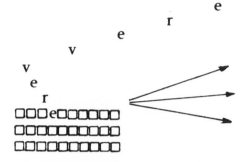

8. Although the second and third Vere's each have a 1 in 361 probability of usefulness separately, the chance that both together will occur in useful positions is 1/361 x 1/361 = 1/130,000 approximately. That is, the chance that each additional Vere will be appropriately located reduces the previous probability by a factor of 1 in 361.

9. Thus the chance that any number (n) of Vere's will all be found usefully positioned is one chance in 361 multiplied by itself that same number (n) times. Applied to the present example there is only 1 chance in 361^{15} or 227,000,000,000,000,000,000,000,000,-000,000,000,000 that the fifteen remaining Vere's will all be found in place to complete the word OXFORD in any given piece of text of the defined size.

The singular improbability of an accidental occurence of this kind can be seen by imagining a little experiment with toothpicks. Suppose a handful of 21 toothpicks were strewn onto a table by dropping them from a convenient height in such a way that they covered an area about six inches wide and two feet long. How many times would one have to strew them on the table at random before they would fall into a pattern forming the six leters of Oxford at a single strewing? It might take more than a lifetime but sooner or later it would be bound to happen. And to just the same degree it is possible that 21 Vere's arranged to spell Oxford will appear by accident in some passage of English text.

The foregoing probability calculation deals with only a part of the whole probability situation. But the uncalculated factors have been handled as definite certainties rather than probabilities, thus giving the devil more than his due. That is to say, where assumptions have been made they were made completely in favor of accidental rather than planned occurrence. If a full, precise calculation were made the resulting figure would be far larger.

At the risk of belaboring an established conclusion, it should be remembered that the letters OXFORD in Sonnets 37-42 are preceded by a similar sequence spelling W SHAKESPEARE and are followed by one spelling VERE, all running in perfect and uninterupted sequence—one letter per Sonnet. It would be fatuous to carry out the calculation for these, or to treat of the even more elobarate acrostic patterns contained in the other Sonnets.

The mathematical aspect should not be concluded without treating another phenomenon of the Sonnets which some may think will invalidate these Vere acrostic patterns. That is this: a thorough search of these texts for every Vere acrostic they contain will reveal a great many extra ones which are not utilized in forming the large toothpick letters. Some of the Sonnets contain two or more extra namesticks for each one that has been utilized in the preceding marked text. Inevitably these extra, or left-over, namesticks provide the opportunity to find other letter formations. It is tempting to conclude that this makes it possible to find almost anything at all with so much raw material to work with. However, the effect of the extra namesticks on the probability calculation is surprisingly small.

A fine-combing of the six Sonnets treated in this chapter has revealed not just twenty-one acrostic Vere's but fifty-eight! Using them, every single letter of the alphabet can be found at least once! If instead of twenty-one toothpicks fifty-eight of them are strewn on the table each time, the chances of accidentally forming OXFORD are greatly increased. In fact, they are increased by a factor of 58/21 raised to the 15th power. That number is 4,110,000. If we divide the previous probability figure by this one, the end result is just to convert the 227 to 55 and to reduce the number of trailing zeros from 36 to 30, thus: 55,000,000,000,000,000,000,-000,000,000,000. The figure still remains astronomical for the improbability of accidentally finding twenty-one Vere's arranged to spell OXFORD in any text passage of the size considered, even though we assume it will have, by inherent accident, fifty-eight Vere's scattered within its borders.

The point that should be emphasized is the difficulty of building a meaningful string of toothpick letters. These acrostics cannot be dismissed by pointing to the frequency with which the four letters VERE and their variants can be found in any newspaper nor to the high concentrations with which they occur in these Sonnets. Even assuming an abundant occurence doubled and re-doubled there remains the need to find each successive namestick in its usable position time-after-time-after-time. For if we should get even as far as ◇ ╳ ╞ ◇ ╠ ╘ and find the last bar of the D missing, there is nothing we can do to manufacture it and the whole message is a nullity.

The marginal acrostics—the "signals"—can be subjected to a similar mathematical assessment. Taking only a few whose relevance to the textual acrostics is especially plain the probability of accidental occurence can be tested by comparison with some other ancient publication of similar size and typography. For example, Ben Johnson's play *The Alchemist* in the quarto edition of 1612 has 88 pages of text composed according to the following 37 line format (the Sonnets fill 65 pages of about 33 lines).[7]

7. *The Alchemist* contains over 1700 Vere acrostics, averaging nearly 20 to the page; but they fail to make anywhere a double line spelling of WILLIAM SHAKESPEARE in uniform orientation, even allowing flagrant "poetic license."

The ALCHEMIST.

Piteoufly coftiue with your pinch'd horne-nofe,
And your complexion, of the *Romane* wafh,
Stuck full of blacke,and melancholique wormes,
Like poulder cornes,fhot, at th'Artillery-yard.
S v b. I wifh,you could aduance your voice, a little.
F A c. When you went pinn'd vp, in the feuerall ragges,
Yo'had rak'd, and pick'd from dunghus, before day,
Your feete in mouldy flippers,for your kibes,
A felt of rugg, and a thin thredden cloake,
That fcarce would couer your no-buttockes. S v b. So S*f*.
F A c. When all your *Alchemye,* and your *Algebra,*
Your *Mineralls,Vegetalls,*and *Animalls,*
Your Coniuring,Cofning,and your dofen of Trades
Could not relieue your corps, with fo much linnen
Would make you tinder, but to fee a fire;
I ga'you count'nance, credit for your Coales,
Your Stilles,your Glaffes, your *Materialls,*
Built you a Fornace, drew you Cuftomers,
Aduanc'd all your blacke Arts ; lent you, befide,
A houfe to practife in. S v b. Your Mafters houfe ?
F A c. Where you haue ftudied the more thriuing skill
Of Bawdry,fince. S v b. Yes, in your Mafters houfe,
You, and the Rats, here, kept poffeffion.
Make it not ftrange. I know,you were one, could keepe
The Buttry-hatch ftill lock'd and faue the chippings,
Sell the dole-beere to *Aqua-vitæ* men,
The which,together with your *Chriftmaffe* vailes,
At Poft, and Paire, your letting out of Counters,
Made you a pretty ftocke fome twenty markes,
And gaue you credit, to conuerfe with cobwebs,
Here, fince your Miftreffe death hath broke vp houfe.
F A c. You might talke foftlier, Raskall. S v b. No, you *Scarabe,*
I'll thunder you, in peeces. I will teach you
How to beware, to tempt a *Fury* 'againe
That carries tempeft in his hand, and voyce.
F A c. The Place has made you valiant. S v b. No, your Clothes.

Thou

These 88 pages can be taken as a reasonable norm for the average occurence of any three letter words in the margin. We may choose as particularly pertinent marginal acrostic signals in the Sonnets:

1. TWO and SLO in Sonnets 51 and 52 where the toothpick letters start to be made with two lines instead of one and where the former pace of one letter per Sonnet slows down.
2. OAF in the second part of the awkwardly divided Sonnet 67 which is repeated again in the first part of divided Sonnet 72 on the next page.
3. FAT occurring three times on the page containing Sonnets 87-89 where the toothpick letters again shift from single line to double line or "fat" construction.

In *The Alchemist* the marginal letters of the entire play contain TWO just four times and contain SLO just once. OAF appears twice and FAT appears nine times. Applying the principles that the chance that one of these will occur on a particular page is the same as that for any other page and that such chance is just the average number of pages per occurence in a representative text, we find the following: (allowing for the ratio of 33 to 37 lines per page between the Sonnets and *The Alchemist*)

TWO has a one in 25 chance of appearing on a Sonnet page.

SLO has a one in 100 chance of appearing on a Sonnet page.

OAF has a one in 50 chance of appearing on a Sonnet page. (But it is significant only if located in a particular 5 or 6 line part which raises the figure to 1 in 275. Its actual occurence in two particular places raises the figure still further to 1 in 275^2 or 75,625.)

FAT has a one in 9 chance of appearing on a Sonnet page. (In fact, it significantly appears 3 times on one page, which raises to figure to 1 in 9^3 or 729.)

The probability that all of the preceding occurrences are accidental is obtained by multiplying these four figures together and comes out at about one chance in 140,000,000,-000. Could any more formidable odds be desired in favor of the proposition that these particular acrostics are not a mere accident of poetic composition but are the intentional product of the most prodigious literary genius of all time? Even in times when the word billion is just a single unit of "coinage" in the fiscal policy of great nations, does one solitary chance out of a hundred and forty billion chances allow much room for speculation that these seven particular marginal acrostics are the result of pure accident? Aren't they instead the intentional tip-offs and confirmations that the internal toothpick letters are also intentional?

The whole of these acrostics can now be weighed against the criteria for legitimacy set out in the first chapter.

1. Do they consistently follow a single system?
2. Does the hidden message make sense throughout?
3. Is it long enough that it could not have occurred fortuitously?
4. Can the same message be derived by different individuals working independently?

The first three questions have obviously affirmative answers. What about independent corroboration?

The single VERE namesticks in the opening and closing lines of Venus and Adonis and of Lucrece give us no hesitation about an affirmative answer. Given the key word, the rest is automatic—there they are. There's no room for any other result. Likewise for the opening and closing "signatures" in the four famous soliloquies. And who could fail to find the marginal acrostics TWO SLO OAF and FAT in the Sonnets on a mere search for any words of three letters or more?

Enough has been said—whether it be a simple VERE running across the first four lines of a poem or be it a complex series of two-lined toothpick letters squeezed into the space of just one Sonnet for each letter—there they are without any special transposition, substitution or any other interpretive manipulations to be performed. Anyone can find them because they stand fully exposed and undisguised in the original and authentic texts. It's just a matter of pointing the particular letters out in the crowd. The only key required is the author's name Vere.

Just as a matter of plain common sense, the sheer number of complete spellings of Shakespeare, Oxford and Vere that are found could not be accidental. Even more confirmatory is the way in which the author kept developing his skill as he went along. After each word pattern was completed he set himself a more difficult task in the next verses and—except for the last try—accomplished it. It is interesting to go back and see how this progressive self-challenge develops.

Sonnet 1 has merely single acrostic Vere's at the start and finish.

The next 21 Sonnets contain only 18 single line letters in random orientation and sometimes two letters are in a single Sonnet and some Sonnets contain none. These latter do contain a single namestick however, either at the beginning or end.

Sonnet 23 is a work apart. Here are four letters, SAIE—or speak—all perfectly formed without resort to any poet's license. Moreover, it is a natural conclusion or reprise to the subject of the Sonnet itself.

Sonnet 24 is a spacer with a leaning pair of crossed namesticks and a single one at the end.

Next he tried to put a complete letter in each Sonnet. Sonnets 25 through 46 contain 22 letter patterns spelling in perfect sequence W SHAKESPEARE—OXFORD—VERE with each Sonnet containing one, and only one, letter. However, 4 out of the 79 namesticks involve poetic license, a reasonable 5%.

After apparently starting to spell DE VERE with perfect namesticks, he dropped the effort in Sonnet 51 for a far grander scheme—the double-lined or block letters. This first WILLIAM SHAKESPEARE in blocks uses 24 Sonnets to make 18 letters ending at Sonnet 75. Skipping the "breather" of single line letters in Sonnets 76 through 86, the series from Sonnet 87 through 110 squeezes 24 block letters into 24 Sonnets with one to spare. By this time the production of symmetrically crossed namesticks for use as fillers or spacers has become almost routine.

The next new goal is to pack six letters into only four Sonnets, 111-114, with again two perfectly crossed pairs of spacers.

In all of the preceding execrises the disposition of the individual letters has been unrestrained. They may lean one way or another, be upside down or be in mirror image. But now comes the block sequence WILLIAM SHAKESPEARE in uniform orientation running through Sonnet 130 with the 18 letters requiring only 15 verses.

Next he set the goal of placing block letters at a rate of one letter per Sonnet. The eleven Sonnets through 141 contain exactly eleven block letters but there is some overlapping. This overlapping is what he set out to eliminate in the next series but was unable to do beyond the first three letters. Nevertheless, the series is complete and winds up a brilliant accomplishment with the final E of the final SHAKE-SPEARE in the final Sonnet.

Just to conceive of a task so prodigious seems fantastic even if woven into mere doggerel. To create such patterns along with the marginal acrostics within these supreme gems of poetry marks a genius even beyond the heights already acknowledged as supreme.

CHAPTER 5
RESPONSE TO TRADITION

Most lovers of Shakespeare exhibit a conditioned reflex to the idea of a concealed authorship. This viewpoint has its own built-in satisfactions and it would be heartless, if it weren't so hopeless, to exhort such minds to seek out the more poignant drama inherent in the true life story of Lord Oxford and his relations to the other great figures of his time. There are, too, those of more comprehensive interests, the experts who know the various heretical theories and are convinced that none of them are valid, and particularly that those purporting to be based upon a secret cipher of some kind are but products of the daft. Reactions of this latter kind rest upon many sound grounds, as the Friedmans have ably demonstrated. But the great majority of serious students of the bard and his works and times will have a number of very relevant questions which seem to require answers that would preclude the Oxford theory and the recognition of these acrostics.

It is usually asserted that Oxford could not be the author because (a) he died in 1604 and (b) *The Tempest* includes several references to a shipwreck on Bermuda which occurred in 1609, and was unknown in England until Sylvester Jourdain arrived there and published the first account of it in 1610. Two other accounts were published, one by Richard Rich and the other by William Strachey. The venerable Dictionary of National Biography (Vol. 17, page 1317, col. 1) is authority for this dating which is accurate enough. The trouble with rejecting Oxford on this evidence is that this was not the first shipwreck on Bermuda which was described in print in England.

The man who published the first story of Bermuda in England was Henry May. He was shipwrecked there in 1593 and returned in 1594 to publish "A Briefe relation of the shipwracke of Henry May 1593." The story was retold by the famous geographical chronicler Richard Hakluyt in 1600, a facsimile of whose relevant pages follows.

THE

THIRD AND LAST

VOLVME OF THE VOY-
AGES, NAVIGATIONS, TRAF-
fiques, and Difcoueries of the *Englifh Nation*, and in
fome few places, where they haue not been, of ftrangers, performed within and before the time of thefe hundred yeeres, to all
parts of the *Newfound* world of *America*, or the *Weft Indies*, from 73.
degrees of Northerly to 57. of Southerly latitude:

As namely to *Engronland*, *Meta Incognita*, *Eftotiland*,
Tierra de Labrador, *Newfoundland*, vp *The grand bay*, the gulfe of *S. Lau-*
rence, and the Riuer of *Canada* to *Hochelaga* and *Saguenay*, along the coaft of *Aram-*
bec, to the fhores and maines of *Uirginia* and *Florida*, and on the Weft or backfide of them
both, to the rich and pleafant countries of *Nueua Bifcaya*, *Cibola*, *Tiguex*, *Cicuic*,
Quiuira, to the 15. prouinces of the kingdome of *New Mexico*, to the
bottome of the gulfe of *California*, and vp the
Riuer of *Buena Guia:*

And likewife to all the yles both fmall and great lying before the
cape of *Florida*, *The bay of Mexico*, and *Tierra firma*, to the coafts and Inlands
of *Newe Spaine*, *Tierra firma*, and *Guiana*, vp the mighty Riuers of *Orenoque*,
Deffekebe, and *Maranmon*, to euery part of the coaft of *Brafil*, to the Riuer of *Plate*,
through the Streights of *Magellan* forward and backward, and to the
South of the faid Streights as farre as 57. degrees:

And from thence on the backfide of *America*, along the coaftes, harbours,
and capes of *Chili*, *Peru*, *Nicaragua*, *Nueua Efpanna*, *Nueua Galicia*, *Culiacan*,
California, *Noua Albion*, and more Northerly as farre as 43. degrees:

Together with the two renowmed, and profperous voyages of Sir *Francis Drake*
and M. *Thomas Canlifh* round about the circumference of the whole earth, and
diuers other voyages intended and fet forth for that courfe.

Collected by RICHARD HAKLVYT *Preacher*, *and fometimes*
ftudent of Chrift-Church in Oxford.

¶ Imprinted at London by *George Bifhop*, *Ralfe*
Newberie, and ROBERT BARKER.
ANNO DOM. 1600.

The laſt of November 1593 Monſieur de la Barbotiere departed from a port called Laguna in Hiſpaniola. The 17 of December next inſuing it was his fortune to haue his ſhip caſt away vpon the Northweſt part of the iſle of Bermuda about midnight; the pilots making themſelues at noone to be to the Southward of the iſland twelue leagues, certified the captaine that they were out of all danger. So they demanded of him their wine of heigth: the which they had. And being, as it ſhould ſeeme, after they had their wine, careleſſe of their charge which they tooke in hand, being as it were drunken, through their negligence a number of good men were caſt away: and I being but a ſtranger among 50 and odde Frenchmen & others, it pleaſed God to appoint me to be one of them that were ſaued, I hope to his ſeruice & glory. We made account at the firſt that we were caſt away hard by the ſhore, being hie clifs, but we found our ſelues ſeuen leagues off: but with our boat and a raft which we had made & towed at our boats ſterne, we were ſaued ſome 26 of vs; among whom were no more Engliſh but my ſelfe. Now being among ſo many ſtrangers, & ſeeing not roome for the one halfe, I durſt neither preſſe into the boat, nor vpon the raft, for feare leſt they ſhould haue caſt me ouerboord, or els haue killed me: ſo I ſtayed in the ſhip which was al- moſt full of water, vntill the captaine being entred the boat, called me vnto him being at hand, for that it ſtood vpon life or death: and ſo I preſently entred, leauing the better halfe of our company to the mercy of the ſea. After this we rowed all the day vntil an houre or two before night yer we could come on land, towing the raft with the boat. When we came on ſhore, being all the day without drinke, euery man tooke his way to ſee if he could finde any: but it was long before any was found. At length one of the pilots digging among a company of weeds found freſh water to all our great comforts, being onely raine water: and this was all the freſh water that we found on ſhore. But there are in this Iſland many fine bayes, wherin if a man did dig, I thinke there might be foſid ſtore of freſh water. This Iſland is diuided all into broken Iſlands: and the greateſt part I was vpon, which might be ſome 4 or 5 miles long, and 2 miles & a halfe ouer; being all woods, as Cedar & other timber, but Cedar is the chiefeſt. Now it pleaſed God before our ſhip did ſplit, that we ſaued our carpenters tooles, or els I thinke we had bene there to this day: and hauing re- couered the aforeſaid tooles we went roundly about the cutting downe of trees, & in the end built a ſmall barke of ſome 18 tun, for the moſt part with tronnels and very few nailes. As for tackling we made a voyage aboord the ſhip before ſhe ſplit, and cut downe her ſhrowds, and ſo we tackled out barke, and rigged her. In ſtead of pitch we made lime, and mixed it with the oile of tortoiſes; and aſſoone as the carpenters had calked, I and another, with ech of vs a ſmall ſticke in our hands, did plaiſter the morter into the ſeames, and being in April, when it was warm and faire weather, we could no ſooner lay it on, but it was dry, and as hard as a ſtone. In this moneth of April 1594, the weather being very hot, we were afrayd our water ſhould faile vs; and therfore made the more haſte away: and at our departure we were conſtrained to make two great cheſts, and calked them, and ſtowed them on ech ſide of our maine maſt, and ſo put in our prouiſion of raine-water, and 13 liue tortoiſes for our food, for our voyage which we intended to Newfoundland. In the South part of this Iſland of Bermuda there are hogs, but they are ſo leane that you can not eat them, by reaſon the Iſland is ſo barren: but it yeeldeth great ſtore of ſowle, fiſh and tortoiſes. And to the Eaſtward of the Iſland are very good harbours, ſo that a ſhippe of 200 tun may ride there land- locked, without any danger, with water enough. Alſo in this Iſland is as good fiſhing for pearles as is any in the Weſt Indies, but that the place is ſubiect to foule weather, as thundering, light- ning and raine: but in April and part of May we had very faire and hot weather. The 11 of May it pleaſed God to ſet vs cleere of the Iſland, to the no little ioy of vs all, after we had liued in the ſame almoſt the ſpace of 5 moneths. And the 20 of May we fell with the land nere to Cape Bri- ton, where we ran into a freſh water riuer, whereof there be many, and tooke in wood, water, and ballaſt. And here the people of the countrey came vnto vs, being clothed all in furs, with the furred ſide vnto their ſkins, & brought with them furres of ſundry ſorts to ſel, beſides great ſtore of wild ducks: ſo ſome of our company hauing ſaued ſome ſmall beads, bought ſome of their ducks. Here we ſtayed not aboue foure houres, and ſo departed. This ſhould ſeeme to be a very good countrey. And we ſaw very fine champion ground, and woods. From this place we ranne for the banke of Newfoundland, whereas we met with diuers, but none would take in a man of vs, vntill it plea- ſed God that wee met with a barke of Falmouth, which receiued vs all for a little time; and with her we tooke a French ſhip, wherein I left capitan de la Barbotier my deere friend, and all his company, and ſtayed my ſelfe aboord the Engliſh barke: and hauing paſſage in the ſame, in the moneth of Auguſt I arriued at Falmouth 1594.

There are two good reasons why this account is the basis of the references in *The Tempest* to Bermuda and a shipwreck there. First, the later account by Jourdain emphasizes that at that time the Bermuda Islands, their frequent storms and hazardous rocks *were matters of common knowledge.*

". . . for the Islands of the Bermudas *as every man knoweth* that hath heard or read of them were never inhabited by Christian or Heathen people but ever esteemed and reputed a most prodigious and enchanted place affording nothing but gusts, stormes, and foule weather which made every navigator an mariner to avoid them as Scylla & Charibidis or as they would shun the Devil; and no man was ever heard to make for the place but as against their wills, they have by stormes and dangerousness of the rocks, *lying seven leagues into the sea,* suffered shipwrecke;"

The particulars are even lifted almost verbatim from Hakluyt's recital: "We made account at the first that we were cast away hard by the shore, being hie cliffs, but we found ourselves seven leagues off." It is impossible to rule out knowledge by Oxford of the Henry May shipwreck. He was a frequent backer of exploratory voyages to the new world and lost a small fortune doing so. He would have every reason to read the fascinating Hakluyt compilations and to be just as familiar with them as was Jordain.

It is an interesting side light that after Oxford's death, the Earl of Southhampton, his putative son and the dedicatee of the poems, was the prime mover of the Virginia Company. Oxford's son-in-law, the Earl of Pembroke, along with Southhampton, headed up the "Royal Council of Virginia" as set up by charter. Strangely, it was the flagship of a fleet of this Company's ships which wrecked on Bermuda in 1609 with Jourdain aboard. How ironic it is that this fact, by an act of careless scholarship, has become a principal bulwark against the recognition of Oxford's true place in the sun.

The second cogent reason why Oxford probably knew of the Henry May shipwreck and used it in *The Tempest* lies in the stark contrast between the conditions on board the two vessels immediately preceding their respective flounders on the rocks. In the Jourdain account the storm had occurred a few days before the wreck and had separated the ship from the rest of the fleet with her seams leaking and all hands manning the pumps around the clock. They became exhausted and hungry and finally gave up all hope. After taking last leave of each other, they were expecting the ship to sink when it wedged itself between two rocks. They were a sober, God-fearing company in imminent expectation of death.

In the Henry May account the crew were in a gay mood only hours before the crack-up and were celebrating with the "wine of height" their success in reaching a certain latitude. This most probably underlies the allusion found in the first scene of *The Tempest* which reads "we are merely cheated of our lives by drunkards" as Alfonso continues his excoriation of the boatswain and his clumsy crew's actions in the storm. This appears on the first page of the first folio of plays and it is on this page that the author has placed his most concentrated acrostic performance. This page is utterly saturated with acrostic "Vere's"—56 of them in 87 lines, all arranged to spell in sequence WILLIAM SHAKESPEARE. He ends the page with an exclamation of relief in the open text "Oh, I have suffered;" presumably in twisting his dramatic text to create the acrostics.

But leaving the acrostics aside, there is no basis whatever for the assertion that Oxford could not have written *The Tempest*. It is absolutely false that the Bermuda shipwreck it is based upon was unknown in England until six years after he died.

No doubt there are other objections to Oxford's claim that are based on the accepted dating of the plays. But the evidence on which modern ideas of play dating are founded is hardly evidence at all. One of the mainstays is the diary of

Henslowe, the theatre manager, in which he has kept a meticulous list of the performances. No one would question its authenticity but does an entry there of a certain play on a certain date carry any weight as to whether the play had not been presented elsewhere earlier? It is specially irrelevant when it is known that plays were frequently revised, retitled, and presented to different kinds of audiences at different times. It is not at all unlikely that a play composed for a royal entertainment would take a long time and go through many revisions before the general public got a chance to see it. The printed versions would come along still later. These had to be entered in the Stationer's Register, but such entries have no significance which would bar completion of a play years before.

Perhaps the weakest reeds on which orthodox chronology rests are the alleged uses by Shakespeare of fragments from the work of others. All of these could as easily be the use by the other writer of a passage from "Shakespeare." If he is assumed to have lived between 1550 and 1604 instead of from 1564 to 1616, then who can say who was the originator of such phrases or passages? A careful review of an accepted chronology table[8] will show nothing which requires a date for any play to have been after Oxford's life. The table, while summarizing a great deal of scholarship, is really entirely speculative so far as setting the actual completion date for a play. As such, the scholar's judgments have been distorted by the apparent need to fit the chronology into the lifetime of the man from Stratford.

Another approach to the riddle of accident or plan lies in the numerous occasions where an acrostic Vere would not be present by the accident of inevitability alone, but its presence, if unplanned, requires a compound accident. That is, in addition to having four words with the required letters in the required vertical alinement, there is present in the acrostic one letter which got there only by a gross misprint. The Sonnets contain a few such which have been pinpointed in the

8. *William Shakespeare. A Study of Facts and Problems.* E. K. Chambers, London 1930, p. 246

178

adjoining notes to numbers 12, 59, 114 and 117. Likewise, several have been found in the plays and some of them involve misprints which have mystified the most eminent scholars and critics. One example will suffice. In the Yale University Press Facsimile of the First Folio—the large book of 36 plays published in 1623—commentator Prouty expresses his perplexity in the following words. (p. xxii).

The Folio text of Much Ado was set up from a copy of the quarto [the single play published in smaller format in 1600], but some interesting changes had been made. The majority of these may be attributed to the compositor of the Folio who corrected some errors but introduced new ones, chiefly through the omission of words; but there are variations which require another explanation. Certain stage directions have been changed and most curious are those in II,3. Here the quarto has "Enter prince, Leonato, Claudio, Musicke." Six lines later occurs this direction: "Enter Balthaser with musicke." The Folio has for the first, "Enter Prince, Leonato, Claudio, and Iacke Wilson," and omits the entrance of Balthaser. The use of the actor's name "Iacke Wilson" is similar to the use of "Kemp" and "Cawley" which we have noted but two questions arise. Why was Balthaser made to come in with the Prince, Leonato and Claudio? And why does the name Wilson appear in the Folio?

The answer is to introduce the following Vere's:

Enter Prince, Leonato, Claudio, and Iacke Wilson.
Prin. Come, shall we heare this musicke?
Claud. Yea my good Lord : how still the euening is,
As husht on purpose to grace harmonie.
Prin. See you where *Benedicke* hath hid himselfe?
Clau. O very well my Lord:the musicke ended,
Wee'll fit the kid-foxe with a penny worth.
Prince. Come *Balthasar*,wee'll heare that song againe.
Balth. O good my Lord,take not so bad a voyce,
To slander musicke any more then once.
Prin. It is the witnesse still of excellency,

Here is a deliberate difference between the Quarto edition (1600) and the Folio (1623). This is not just a printshop mistake. Its nature raises the question of which was actually composed by the author first. The Quarto version, if first as universally assumed, would lack the acrostic Vere's which use the *e* in Jacke Wilson and the *w* in Worth, the latter because the stage direction "Enter Balthaser with Musicke" intervenes between it and the *e* in heare. It would then require that someone, author or reviser, had noticed the acrostic possibilities, including the marginal signals and links, (which then must have been accidents in the Quarto) and tinkered the stage directions to produce the acrostic Vere's for the Folio edition.

It is at least as probable that the Folio text, with all acrostics, was in existence, either as manuscript or possibly printed privately, before the Quarto was published. The tinkering of this (the Folio) text to *eliminate* the acrostics for the Quarto publication would be an equally if not more plausible explanation. Oxford was under the strongest possible constraint to keep his authorship of the plays concealed and very probably was ordered not to permit even anonymous publication. Sonnet 23 stresses his enforced silence.

But there was no constraint to prevent greedy booksellers from trying to pirate the texts of the plays unscrupulously. How galling to him to find that in spite of his compliance with orders his plays were beginning to appear in print as "stolen and surreptitious" copies (the "bad" Quartos) and quite inferior in content to the versions he had been carefully perfecting over several years. How naturally and urgently would he wish to put the proper texts into readers' hands. But these were filled with acrostics which, if discovered in the wrong quarters, would mean the Tower and possibly the block. The answer was to release to the printer a manuscript with the acrostics garbled by misprints, rearrangement of lines, shifting from verse to prose, and using long passages of continuous italics. Differences of this kind be-

tween Folio and good Quarto editions of various plays are
both common and the source of much scholastic bewilder-
ment. The development of additional instances in the plays
is beyond present scope, however. The point is raised here
merely to show the very real possibility that the Folio was
not printed from earlier Quartos, prompt books and the like
but could have been set from a carefully executed manuscript arranged an a column-for-column, line-for-line basis.
And that manuscript would have been in gestation for a
decade or more in 1600.

This leads to another valid query, this time from the
bibliography specialists. How is it possible for anyone to set
down on paper by hand a text which can be set up in type
without losing most of the letter alinements which make up
the internal acrostics? Here is a typical Elizabethan manuscript which happens to be a part of a scene from *Titus Adronicus*. The first eighteen lines are exactly like the first
Folio but the rest is a departure. It was penned by Henry
Peacham in 1595 and contains six acrostic Vere's. These are
accidental because there are no marginal signals or links.

If now we turn to the corresponding lines in type in the Folio, it is remarkable how closely the same letters line up.

```
    Iun.  Stay Romaine Bretheren, gracious Conqueror,
  Victorious Titus, rue the teares I shed,
  A Mothers teares in passion for her sonnes:
  And if thy Sonnes were euer deere to thee,
  Oh thinke my sonnes to bees deere to mee.
  Sufficeth not, that wee are brought to Rome
  To beautifie thy Triumphs, and returne
  Captiue to thee, and to thy Romaine yoake,
  But must my Sonnes be slaughtred in the streetes,
  For Valiant doings in their Countries cause?
    O! If to fight for King and Common-weale,
    Were piety in thine, it is in these:
? Andronicus, staine not thy Tombe with blood.
  Wilt thou draw neere the nature of the Gods?
  Draw neere them then in being mercifull,
  Sweet mercy is Nobilities true badge,
  Thrice Noble Titus, spare my first borne sonne.
    Tit.  Patient your selfe Madam, and pardon me.
  These are the Brethren, whom you Gothes beheld
  Aliue and dead, and for their Bretheren slaine,
  Religiously they aske a sacrifice:
  To this your sonne is markt, and die he must,
```

This was not an intentional phenomenon certainly, but it illustrates that it would not be too difficult to transfer from manuscript to printed page the individual letter positions necessary to show the Vere arcostics.

Fortunately, there are examples of Oxford's handwriting extant and these span almost his whole life. Here is a letter he wrote in French when he was only thirteen and a half.

182

His script is, at this early age, very regular, with the letters
formed individually and of uniform size much like printer's
type.

Monsieur treshonorable

Monsieur i'ay receu voz lettres, plaines d'humanité et courtoysie, & fort resemblantes
a vostre grand amour et singuliere affection enuers moy, comme vrais enfans
deuement procreez d'une telle mere. pour la quelle ie me trouue de iour en iour
plus tenu a v. h. voz bons admonestemens pour l'obseruation du bon ordre
selon voz appointemens, ie me delibere, dieu aidant, de garder en toute ac... ...
comme ensie que ie cognois et considere tendre specialement a mon propre
bien et profit, usant en cela l'aduis et authorité de ceux qui sont aupres
de moy. la discretion desquels i'estime si grande (s'il me conuient parler
quelque chose a leur aduantage) qui non seulement ilz se porteront
selon qu'un tel temps le requiert, mais que plus est feront tant que
ie me gouuerne selon que vous aues ordonné et commandé. Quant a l'ordre
de mon estude pour ce que il requiert un long discours a l'expliquer par
si menu, et le temps est court a ceste heure, ie vous prie affectueuse-
ment m'en excuser pour le present. vous asseurant que par le premier
passant ie le vous feray sçauoir bien au long. cependant ie prie adieu
vous donner santé.

Edward Oxenford

Thirty-seven years later he was still writing in clear,
uniform letters much like the folio type.

Another letter a few years earlier indicates that it was written (possibly by a secretary) with some form of line guide since the lines are perfectly straight, horizontal and equally spaced.

It is not too difficult to imagine Oxford putting his master-pieces to paper in this almost perfect handwriting—"with scarce a blot" as Ben Jonson said—and knowing that it will come out in print without loss of the ingenious acrostics he has somehow woven into them. As Speed says in *The Two Gentlemen of Verona*, "Oh excellent device, was there ever heard a better/ that my master being scribe/ to himself should write the letter?" (That is, to his own name in acrostic—which he would put down on the page first—he should write the lines of the play.)

In spite of careful penmanship, not all of the acrostic patterns woven into the plays survived the trials of the print shop and its apparently unsuspecting compositors. Some of the most intricate patterns occur in places where recent bibliographic studies show a mystifying hiatus in the time sequence of printing the consecutive pages. Both Shroeder in *The Great Folio of 1623* and Hinman in *The Printing and Proof Reading of the First Folio of Shakespeare* have traced in utmost detail the minute nicks and dents in individual pieces of type and in the brass rule strips used to form the border lines. In this way the sequence of typesetting and printing in Jaggard's print shop has been reconstructed with uncanny certainty. Both authors have found many places where the normal sequence of quires was interrupted for a few pages, then continued on for a distance, only to go back later and print the pages that were skipped. Logically, this would have been done to correct printers' errors in the pages skipped. But both authors agree that the reprinted pages are so full of both printers' and proof readers' mistakes that this does not explain the abnormality.

> "A peculiar attitude toward the Romeo text would seem to have prevailed in the printing-house during the preparation of this play for the Folio. —as if the compositor and proof-reader alike, though having their jobs to do, were somehow unable to discharge their appointed tasks with their usual conscientiousness."—Hinman

Similarly, Shroeder finds the anomalies so puzzling as to suggest

> "the presence of a critical intelligence coming between the compositors and the line of least resistance, though who he was, what he had in mind and where he was at other times are questions whose answers do not yet appear."

Whoever that "critical intelligence" may have been, he or she surely was in on the secret of the acrostics and was proofreading the print shop output to assure proper letter alinements. The process apparently took a few days and by the time a bad quire was discovered (galley proofs were not used in those times) the printing had proceeded several pages beyond. This meant re-setting the type for the bad quire and running off new sheets to replace the cancelled ones. Thus, the minute nicks and bends in type and rules which had come about while the printers ran blithely on past the bad quires would show up in the replacement pages.

A convincing confirmation of this is found in a group of the Romeo pages which were printed in very abnormal order. —Shroeder says "The staggered printing of Romeo stands at the head of these [questions]." Here is the pattern of Vere acrostics to be found in thirteen successive columns of one group of those pages. There are about three hundred acrostic Vere's used to form this pattern.

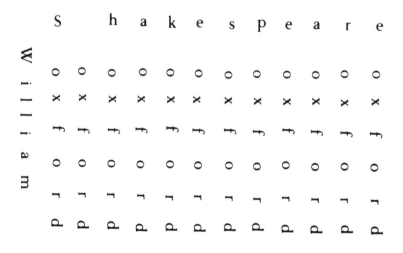

Romeo and Juliet contains also a thinly veiled reference to the acrostic system. When Juliet's mother tries to interest

her in the favored suitor, Paris, she compares him to a book
—hardly a romantic metaphor to a girl of fourteen.

"Read ore the volume of young Paris face
and find delight, writ there with Beauties pen,
　　(Read over the volume and find delight.)
Examine every severall liniament
　　(Look at every single line.)
And see how one another lends content
　　(See how each lends content to the next.)
And what obscured in this faire volume lies
Find written in the margent of his eyes."
　　(The obscure messages are found by
　　looking in the margin.)

Knowing the Shakespearean penchant for word play it
is not hard to read a double meaning into this passage. In
fact, the evident meaning hardly makes sense. How can a
careful examination of the liniaments of Paris' face reveal
one liniament lending content (or perhaps contentment) to
another? And why look at the edges of his eyelids? What
could be hidden there? The whole passage skirts the border
of absurdity unless it were meant to have a double meaning.

Similarly in Cymbeline, Lord Oxford has almost openly
described the lamentable situation that his dalliance in the
royal bed has eventually brought down upon him.

　　　　　　　"I have belyed a Lady,
The Princesse of this Country; and the ayre on't
Revengingly enfeebles me, or could this Carle,
A very drudge of Natures, have subdu'de me
In my profession? Knighthoods, and Honors borne
As I weare mine) are titles but of scorne."

This becomes literal autobiography if only "belyed" is
read as—lain with—and "ayre" is read as—heir—. Carle is
an archaic word for a country yokel; meaning here the one
from Stratford.

But passages of this kind, while persuasive to the dis-
cerning reader, can never be taken as firmly conclusive.

There is no way to determine mathematically or by other logical discipline that the secondary meaning was intended by the author. Each reader is thrown upon his own subjective judgment. But the acrostic patterns, in contrast, do lend themselves to a determination, positively and by long accepted methods of evaluating chance, whether they could or could not be accidentally present. Thus tested, their presence turns out to be intentional by an astronomical preponderance.

They are found in the original edition of the Sonnets themselves—the primary source. This is the Bard himself speaking—after nearly four centuries. The voice that was so harshly muffled by a tyrant queen has finally burst its gag and confirms what has been surmised by a growing body of observers. It is the voice of the Earl of Oxford—speaking fresh words here and now. Though he hasn't been around for quite a while, we are privileged to catch for the first time some of what he was trying so hard to shout through the wall of censorship. It's a phase of immortality that transcends even the legacy of his writings, as they have heretofore been known and enjoyed. It has the quality of being present and looking over your shoulder. And then we realize afresh that the divine hand has been there all the time—as it always is.

CHAPTER 6

IN SUMMARY

Here at last is the "documentary evidence" that both the heretical and the orthodox sides of the authorship controversy have lacked. The heretics have always pointed to the absence of any writing of the times which shows a connection between the Stratford man and the Shakespeare works. And they are correct in insisting that all allusions which refer to "Shakespeare," with or without the "William," can be taken to mean anyone by that name whether it be his real name or an assumed one. Likewise, the orthodox have rightly discounted the profuse, and often abstruse, parallels between events in the life of Oxford, Bacon, Derby, Rutland, or whoever, and the actions of the plays upon which most heretical theories are founded.

How all this will eventually affect the future study of Elizabethan history and literature will not be conjectured here. The evidence is now submitted to be weighed by the jury of public opinion. The objections of opposing counsel have been refuted, and overruled. It remains merely to hear counsel's summary of the case.

Queen Elizabeth The First and the "establishment" of her time stand charged with conspiring to assassinate the name and memory of Edward de Vere, a peer of the realm and the acknowledged master genius of English literature. This, the seventeenth bearer of a distinguished title going back nearly to the Norman Conquest was reared in the ideals of feudalism. His loyalty and devotion to Queen and country were in-bred from childhood. His dedication to the truth was matched only by his unerring ability to reveal it in the most penetrating language. Through his love of the dramatic arts he addressed his genius to the creating of a heritage

189

of literature to stir men's souls throughout the ages.

At first a brilliant ornament to the court, accomplished in musicianship, sports, and courtly repartee, his sparkling wit was an attractive foil to the Queen's own surpassing intellect. His skill with poetry and his talent for writing and producing entertainments for the court kept him for several years a first rank favorite of the Queen. By wit and insight into the frailties of the Lords and Ladies, and even of the Queen herself, he made his plays a steady and often uproarious source of court amusement.

Elizabeth was one of the last absolute monarchs. Her father, in casting off the Papal allegiance, had freed her from any restraint but her own will and what she saw of God's will. She held her courtiers in a domination no less complete than master over slave. They were royal property, body, mind, and soul. This daughter of lecherous Henry VIII and the seductive Ann Boleyn was no vestal iceberg, but was endowed by inheritance with the instincts of a Cleopatra and a lifetime of opportunity to exercise them with impunity. Besides Lord Oxford's service as master mind of the court "revels," which were actually plays, she demanded service of more personal nature. When nearly forty and he but twenty-two, a boy was born of their union. He was secretly placed with the Earl of Southhampton and his countess in place of a child of theirs. He grew up to become the third Earl, the one to whom the early poems are so intimately dedicated.

To discourage any thoughts of Oxford becoming the royal consort, the Queen and William Cecil, her faithful Counselor, arranged his marriage to his fifteen year old daughter, Anne Cecil. The wily Cecil thus maneuvered an alliance with an aristocratic house. He also persuaded Elizabeth to elevate him to the nobility in order that his daughter might qualify for such a marriage. The now Lord Burleigh had again shown his mastery of the art of political manipulation and fastened himself for life upon a place near the head of the line for Royal favor.

Lord Oxford, in Burleigh's eyes, was no longer an obstacle to the diplomatic game which the Queen was playing —a game of balancing France against Spain through her possible marriage into the ruling house of one country or the other. Such an alliance would bring Britain back into the spiritual domain of the Pope and end the heresy that was flourishing there to the very real chagrin of both France and Spain. But that was only the bait which she skillfully dangled between the two great powers to keep them from combining forces against her. Meanwhile, she nurtured England's development into a world power. If Lord Oxford were to lay claim to a place in the line of English succession for his and Elizabeth's natural son, then the diplomatic game would be up so far as the Queen's prospects for a continental marriage were concerned. He must be muzzled, collared, and leashed, as the Queen and her council saw things. It was no problem to keep Oxford silent about the affair so far as any direct revelation was concerned. State secrets were kept secret merely by tyrannical threats of force which could be, and frequently was, exercised through barbaric forms of punishment and torture.

For the Queen, matters were quite satisfactory, and would have continued so throughout the years but for one thing. Oxford was becoming a major creator of entertainment for the court through the increasingly clever plays he wrote and produced. These derived much of their impact from their topical nature as Elizabeth delighted in watching the foibles of the aristocracy, including her own, limned and lampooned. But this was not intended for public consumption. As the number of these private stage hits increased, word of their existence spread, and the plays were gradually introduced to the general public. Thus, it again became necessary to put Lord Oxford under binding restraint. To conceal his connection with these plays, lest their obvious relevance to court personages and events should receive the stamp of authenticity, he was forced into a most inviolable undertaking whereby his identity as the author would not be exposed. Instead, he chose the pseudonym William Shakespeare to identify their author.

Thus was born a gargantuan ruse destined to endure for centuries and to deceive the literate public of the entire world. It was methodically abetted by Lord Burleigh's complete distortion of the record as he left it to posterity. By this alias of duress, coupled with a chance resemblance to the name of an unlettered litigious opportunist from Stratford, the world has for over three hundred years been duped into the worship of an idol of clay. No other of the strange anomalies of Elizabeth's reign compares with this injustice dealt to her most illustrious subject.

To Edward de Vere belonged every bit of the adulation that has fallen on the Stratford man, and more beside. The personal tragedies he encountered, the scurrilous treatment he later received from the Queen, and above all his unrealized hopes to see their son succeed to the throne, are true life drama more poignant than any of the plays he wrote. Even those intimate revelations of his innermost feelings, in the Sonnets, could not openly hint of these events.

Perhaps the ruse was justified by the demands of a stripling nation struggling for the prize of empire. Perhaps the misdirected idol worship of the intervening centuries is to be commended for its zeal—although not for its discernment. And perhaps the truth of the matter, which Lord Oxford so skillfully wove into the text of his works, can soon be generally acknowledged.

Many students of the problem have outlined the shape of the conspiracy. Looney's superb piece of literary detective work first exposed the probability that Oxford was the real Shakespeare. The many parallel characteristics of Oxford's early signed poetry and of that later appearing under pseudonym; the almost perfect match between Oxford's personal traits and those which the Shakespeare plays reveal about their author; all have provided most telling circumstantial

evidence. The Ogburns developed a further wealth of material, particularly the part that Burleigh played in concealing
the true picture from posterity. With the help of many others,
most of the jig saw pieces have been put into place. The
picture thus revealed has lacked only the stamp of an authentic tie to the documents of the times.

Here at last is that tie, the proof in the original Shakespeare texts that Edward de Vere, Seventeenth Earl of Oxford, was the genius who gave the world its most magnificent
literary treasures, and that he could not openly reveal that
truth. Ladies and gentlemen of the jury, if you are to declare
the truth, which is the very meaning of the word "ver-dict,"
you must hold the defendants guilty. Thereby must die what
has been perhaps the most durable deception of all time; and
the name and true identity of history's master mind of letters
receive its just acknowledgement.

INDEX

Verity Press

Southfield, Michigan 48075